Book Two
Religion

Second Edition

By K Kobayashi

This book is the exposition of religion of the human kind, focusing the attention to Buddhism and Christianity, through the author's eyes.

Strictly Literary™,
PO Box 242,
Scarborough, Queensland, Australia, 4020.
www.strictlyliterary.com
Phone: 0413 004 138
First published by Strictly Literary, Australia, in 2016

First Published 2016

Second Edition 2020

ISBN: 978-0-9923297-6-1

The author K Kobayashi is issuing the following series of books:

Book One *Idealism and Materialism*
Book Two *Religion*
Book Three *Communism*
Book Four *The Third Prophecy*
Book Five *The Sexual Laws*

Though the series is a coherent unit with the unified purpose, each book is designed to be read independently from the others. The first three books are preparing for the proposal and the last book is augmenting the proposal. His core proposition is in Book Four *The Third Prophecy*; in fact it can be expressed in one simple sentence 'To love a child is not to make one'.

He proposes the love which is the most beautiful and the strongest the humans will ever know; and unless this love is stronger than the love between the sexes the proposal does not make any sense. People imbued with this love gladly discard everything else including their sweethearts. As the concession to an idealised state of being single the sweethearts, unmarried, may remain friends to have sex with precaution against pregnancy. Buddhists and Christians have always taught their adherents to be single all their life. The author firmly believes that marriage has been the greatest curse of the human race. Men and women suffered tremendously through marriage all these millenniums still they could not work out the way out. Only the love of the Third Prophecy leads the ordinary people to stay out of marriage with the unwavering conviction.

This love when adopted by an individual will fulfil what the first (idealism; and religion as crystallisation of idealism) and second (materialism; and communism as an extreme form of materialism) prophecies promised but did not deliver in full to the humans and human societies. This love when adopted by a society as a whole will fulfil not only the first and second prophecies to the full but also will solve many serious problems the humans have had all these millenniums as well as the humans may have in the future. The acceptance of this new way of life by the bulk of the population will result in hugely reduced population with the predominantly beneficial results to humans. This leaves one serious problem for the ordinary single men and women, that is, how to solve their sexual problem. The author proposes the solution of this problem mainly addressed to single men in Book Five *The Sexual Laws*. He expounds the solution getting the idea from 'mind only' developed by the Buddha; the mind only concept is explained in Book Two *Religion*.

The author wants to prove beyond reasonable doubt that the arrival of the societies dominated by this new way of life is inevitable in the future provided the humans act according to the survival instinct as they have done all these millenniums. Since his message is contrary to the people's way of thinking in the past and present, he thinks that the ordinary people at present do not comprehend the message of the Third Prophecy, and it will take one century for the general public to fully appreciate its teaching and live according to its creed.

Contents

Introduction **1**

Chapter 1 Birth of Religion **5**
Section 1 Emergence of Concept of Divinity 5
Section 2 Various Religions 11
Section 3 Universality of Divinity 38

Chapter 2 Judaism-Christianity-Islam **52**
Section 1 Quiddity of Judaism-Christianity-Islam 52
Section 2 Aboriginal People of Australia 63

Chapter 3 Buddhism **67**
Section 1 Buddhist Doctrines and their Development 67
Section 2 Mind Only (or Emptiness): Haecceity of Buddhism 80
Section 3 Similar Concepts as Mind Only (or Emptiness) in History 97

Reference List with Text Citations Marked **102**

Index **108**

Introduction

I think I got to know the core theories of Christianity after several years of fairly intensive study in my youth, though I did not have any previous knowledge on any sort of religion. After 40 years, my approach to the Bible is not substantially different from my understanding acquired at the initial stage. I still hold much the same opinions as to what the Christian life should be, though I have gained further experience about life. As the result of my life experience my understanding of the Bible has drastically changed in one respect, which I am to describe in the paragraphs to follow. The things that have happened to me in the light of my Christian faith are so extraordinary that I don't think it is possible to convey them effectively to readers with all my descriptive skills. Besides, I am sure my religious experiences do not interest readers, and hence I keep my personal life to a minimum in the text.

I now hold a view which I rejected outright at my youth. Unlike the New Testament, the Old Testament presents the anthropomorphic God with human emotions. The latter Testament says that God will send out sicknesses, accidents, natural disasters, poor harvests and all the hosts of other calamities if people do not heed the words of God. In fact this was the way the ancients understood their life the world over. The ancient Egyptians, Jews, Greeks, Chinese all strongly indicated and upheld the notion. I used to think that the ancients held that notion in the absence of scientific ideas and I dismissed it as nonsense. I categorically did not believe in the miracles in the Old and New Testaments. This notion matched with my conviction that God did not preside over the human affairs and was simply a metaphor of the phenomena of the universe, though nobody could escape from the judgement of God.

In the Christian gathering I attended in my youth, I clearly remember the middle aged man who insisted that all the calamities above mentioned come from God in the deep and correct understanding of the Bible. I dismissed his claim at the time. In the light of all my unbelievable experiences in my subsequent life which I could not explain how and why they happened with all my intelligence, I have come to think that he may be right. Many of, or I would rather say, all of my wishes, which I genuinely held in my heart, was realised later in my life. Some people who took upper hands with deception and won over me came to grief in due course; some got sick, some lost their jobs and some even died. It's not that I witnessed misfortunes of the opponents who lied badly every time; in some case we were separated just after the event and did not get to know what happened to them. Further in my patient struggles against mighty adversaries incredible events defying logic took place and I eventually prevailed over them. The Bible says that anybody who stirs the strife with the faithful will fall. In this modern age if I say that the natural disasters such as earthquakes and tsunamis come from God, people may laugh at me. I now suspect, though not totally convinced, that they may happen as a consequence of human sins. We still have to explain why the innocent people have to suffer as the consequence of the sins of the majority of people in the same community.

The biblical authors must have contrived some miracles and stories—I do not believe this statement goes against the biblical teachings—to impart their belief in God (Truth), which we should understand in the same light as the fairy tales.

On the other side of the globe, harmony prevailed in the Confucian state of China, and the Confucian authorities attributed the various calamities (natural and human) to the failure to maintain Confucian ideologies.

What happened to my life in the context of the biblical teachings are like the experimental data in the field of science. They are true to me until I die, regardless of what theories people may propose. I have some uncertainties as to which stories were factual and which stories were contrived in the Bible though there is no denying that it is a remarkable book. Even the biblical scholars place strong doubts on some of the figures presented in the Bible. In fact the theories must conform to the experiences of my life to be of any value to me. Since my own experience is the base of my faith, the argument that God exists or not is irrelevant to me.

I also studied Buddhism with a great deal of curiosity. I spent far greater time reading the Buddhist canons than the Bible. Some of the Buddhist theories such as the Four Noble Truths and the Eightfold Paths were not difficult to understand. However, the concepts of both Mind Only (or Emptiness) and No-Ego were beyond my comprehension initially: they were so different from what I had believed in and from what I had learned from the mass media. I have come to comprehend to some extent the above mentioned theories after spending so much time and effort. I judge these concepts theoretically correct but it is hard to put them into practice. I strongly feel that the fact I resolved to write a book indicates that I am not practising these concepts. A true Buddhist would not write a book and in fact the Buddha and Christ did not leave any books.

Confucianism appealed to me at some stage but after so many years it ceased to satisfy my intellectual curiosity to the extent that it could become the models by which I should shape my daily life. I read the sayings of the ancient to classical Greek philosophers with an absorbing interest. I also read the Qur'an and the religious doctrines of many other faiths. I had to study all these subjects to be able to write a book on religion.

A few people criticised me that I learned various religions without focus: they told me to choose one of them for an intensive learning. As a matter of fact, I have never had a dilemma that I had to choose one religion over another. My curiosity was so strong that I did not allow myself confined in one discipline.

Nobody can deny that religion has played a major role in forming human destiny through history. Chapter 1 of this book tries to fathom how religions came into existence in a general term rather than on individual religions, the latter being the usual approach in dealing with the subject. Even in the treatise of comparative religions readers will find, normally, that it treats each religion separately with some cross references. The critiques may argue that unless we qualify the religious teachings by place and time, they do not make any sense. Possibly people, writers as well as readers, feel that only the presentation of this kind make some sense and the various religions dealt together in one heading would be nonsensical, though I adopt the latter approach in this chapter (and even extending to this entire book), emphasising the uniformity of the religious developments for virtually all the races in the world.

Though the various religions of the world have different presentations, the similar motives and concepts have impressed me, considering that vastly differing peoples conceived them under widely varying environs. Religion was one of the means of survival for the humans. Buddhism and Judaism have particularly fascinated me over the years and became the main focus of study in this book, and I quote them most frequently in the other parts of this series of books. I have come to believe that these two systems of thoughts stand up well to satisfy people of today and still hold bright promise for the future of mankind. They are superbly elaborated doctrinally, many authors (Buddhists, Judaists and Christians) having contributed for their developments. Also these stand out among the other strands of thoughts in emphasising the importance of being single rather than married, which suits my development of the theme of Book Four *The Third Prophecy*.

The Buddha's life had a strong resemblance to Christ's. The Buddha (or Christ) reinterpreted the traditional Hindu (or Jewish) teachings and both, going against the tradition, insisted the equality of all human beings rejecting the racial element to become the initiators of the world religion. They taught that the primary concern of the people should be the adherence to the religious truths rather than to the race. They were in fact religious reformers. The Buddha and Christ spread the truths in the colloquial spoken language, not in written and not in scholarly language, and especially their similes were superb. The similarity of the two religions they taught goes further. The Jewish majority rejected Christianity which developed from Judaism, and adhered to Judaism. Likewise the Hindu majority adhered to Hinduism embracing the caste system, and rejected Buddhism which developed from Hinduism and did not recognise the caste system.

It is needless to say that the opinions expressed in this book are only my interpretations, and in some respects differ from the views of authorities who tend to look at the subjects from the different angles. In this book, a historical account throws light as to how and why the religions came to dominate practically all human societies. Religious dominance in the Western world seemed complete in the Middle Ages: in the thirteenth century the power (spiritual and temporal) of the papacy under Innocent III unquestionably reached its peak, whereas Buddhism did not have such a degree of influence in the Eastern society outside the Buddhist orders. Confucianism which seemed rather an ethical teaching than religion had a strong hold on the Chinese society in different ways from the European societies as I explain in 'Introduction to Series', Book One. Upon the above premise, I emphasise that even people in the European medieval era were not so different from people today in their religious consciousness, as we might imagine otherwise. The following incident highlights the above argument symbolically:

> Innocent III, greatest of popes, died in Perugia and his body was left alone unwashed in the church. During the night, thieves stripped it of its precious vestments and left it almost naked and stinking in the church. (Randall 1976, p. 78)

After all, when viewed as a percentage of conscious minds, the religions, however imaginative and truthful they might have been, have not had total hold on any human society, whose reasons I present in Book Four *The Third Prophecy*.

Though the religious thoughts played important roles in virtually all the communities of the world in the process of their development, the main focus in this book is Buddhism and Christianity. The main focus of comparison in Book One *Idealism and Materialism* is China proper and Western Europe. Historically Confucianism was the state cult of China proper, and Christianity, the guiding faith of Europe. Instead of Confucianism Buddhism occupies the dominant position together with Christianity in this book. Buddhism and Christianity are the doctrinally most developed and are apt to be called the world religion together with Islam. When I say Christianity in terms of doctrines, I include Judaism and Islam since the theoretical foundations of these faiths are the same originating in Judaism as I explain in 'Introduction to Series', Book One; and also in the text to follow.

Chapter 1 Birth of Religion

Section 1 Emergence of Concept of Divinity

Primitive people formed a family or a band during savagery and engaged in hunting and gathering. The purpose of grouping is not hard to guess. It was cooperation for hunting animals, gathering food and defending themselves against wild animals and enemy humans. If abstractly expressed, the cohabitation was for survival and in fact survival is the ultimate aim of cohabitation even in the modern society, though the meanings of the survival may be quite different.

The first groupings were not much different from the mammalian packs we observe in the wild today. The animals have a definite code of conducts, and punish or expel from the pack a member which breaks the code. In the similar way for the primitive humans it would not have taken long to realise that they had to have a code of behaviours within the group for the group's harmonious life or even for their sheer existence. It would have been impossible for a group (a pair, a family or a band) to live together without certain restraints. The code or restraints I am referring to is of moral nature rather than of social mores. Obviously experience rather than speculation formed the moral codes. In the first place, the primitive people did not speculate much with their underdeveloped brains. In the second place, they did not have any judgement criteria other than their direct knowledge and feelings: they did not communicate beyond their speech--articulate speech came into existence in the late Palaeolithic Age--and they did not write or read at this stage of development. In the third place, only the results of their experience were useful for their existence and survival. Hence when we observe the group of animals or humans exists, we can assume that the crude moral restrictions are already in place among its members.

The primary school children do not know why they have to learn. The teachers and the parents know from their own experience that the children must learn certain things for the preparation for life. This relationship is similar to God and the devotees in the Christian theology. Many devotees do not know why they have to behave in a certain way and later in their life they realise that was the case. God or Truth is a vast experience a large number of thinkers accumulated over the millenniums.

As the primitive people came out of savagery they formed a tribe and engaged in farming. They had to enforce the criminal laws, though unwritten, vigorously to maintain the law and order within the tribe, otherwise the tribe could have disintegrated, and thus the chance of survival of the tribe as a whole and consequently of the members would have greatly diminished. Hence, the tribesmen meted out the proper punishments on any infringements. The tribesmen whipped, jailed, banished, killed or inflicted other punishments on the offenders depending on the nature of the offences. The tribesmen delivered the punishments only within the tribe and we can also surmise that they punished, condoned or even encouraged any breaches against the neighbouring tribesmen according to the relationship of the two tribes. At the time of open hostility, the penal codes ceased to have any meaning between warring tribes and the breaches became the norm, as it is today between two nations at war. By the definition of war, the participants stole whatever they needed, killed the enemy and played tricks in whatever manner, totally ignoring the moral codes. When one tribe conquered the other, it is more often than not that the conquered kept their own penal codes, rather than adopting the penal codes of the conquerors.

One principle can hold without reservation: People needed religions as well as moral codes for their survival and both became parts of the human psyche. Hence people universally practised them the world over with some differences which may appear to be odd to the other people but once understood they seem natural. Another principle may be intermingling of the religious traditions. The maxim that everything is in continuous flux applies, naturally, to human natures and religions. No religious thinking existed without changes, resulting from new spiritual questions, borrowings, symbiosis or elimination (Eliade 1978, p. 191).

Many of the religious ideas through the history of human kinds intermingled; they ran into and were derived from the other religions. For example, Christianity absorbed a large measure of Greek, particularly stoic, philosophy (Marx & Engels 1970, p. 373). Also, Zoroastrianism influenced the formation of Christianity (Spielvogel 1991, p. 54). The haloes around the Buddha and Christ which appeared first time at the beginning of the Christian era derived from the shining halo of Ahura Mazda (Eliade 1982, p. 216). Further, Buddhism found its point of departure and inspiration for the creation of Chan (Ch'an) Buddhism in Daoism (Taoism), and Neo-Confucianism established its theory of cosmic structure on the mode of Daoism (Sharma 1993, p. 280).

Logically speaking there must be originators of the religions as for any other forms of cultures. Syncretism is an immemorial and abundantly documented phenomenon in the religion. It played an important role in the formation of not only Hittite, Greek and Roman religions but in the religions of Israel, Mahayana Buddhism and Daoism. The surprising creativity characterises the syncretism of the Hellenic and Roman periods. (Eliade 1982, p. 277) At some stage of the human development the religion had a firm hold on the people as we can see today that materialism (material culture and the desire for wealth) has the strongest hold on the daily life of the people.

I have noticed over the years that idealism is remarkably similar all over the world. People who are familiar with Greek philosophy, Confucianism, Judaism, Christianity, Islam and Buddhism would note that the ethical precepts similar to the Ten Commandments, also known as Decalogue, of Judaism appear in all these faiths. People certainly expressed them suitable to the local conditions determined by their traditional cultures. Idealism is the fundamental laws of human existence. The main component of idealism is morals, virtues or ethics and in practice exhibited as the precept 'Love thy neighbour'.

The Buddha laid down five rules of conduct as minimum requirements for the lay people:

- Do not kill.
- Do not steal.
- Avoid sexual excesses.
- Do not lie.
- Abstain from intoxicants.

Buddhism repeats the following precept in many sutras: Avoid the three fold base cravings of lust, avarice and hate. The Bible also mentions this teaching in many of its books.

Sabbath of Judaism, Christianity and Islam may be an exceptional concept to the above general rule and I cannot find any parallels to the idea of Sabbath in any other faiths in the sense that Sabbath is a weekly holy day. The holy days in other faiths are normally yearly events, that is, they are based on seasons of the year. The festivals were seasonal such that people, after reaping the harvests, can enjoy themselves using the spare time. Ironically, Sunday, which is Sabbath of Christians, is regarded as a holiday virtually all over the world today.

Though the moral precepts probably came into existence for practical necessity of cohabitation, their universality and irrefutability must have made the ancient people feel that they were beyond human control and came from overwhelming premise of God. The ancient people did not know and we the modern people still don't understand the reasons behind, but when people transgressed the moral bounds, the evils came upon them without fail, personally, or on a group of people as a whole. People ascribed the phenomena to the works of gods or God, in the absence of clear comprehension.

The central theme of Confucianism is ren (jen) which I render in this series of book as 'Love thy neighbour'. This precept runs through the Bible, and it repeatedly denounces the contemporary people for not adhering to this ordinance. For example; I found one upright man among a thousand, but not one upright woman among them all (Ecclesiastes 7:28).

Aristotle said that the highest aim of life is to attain happiness through morals. Menander said that the highest good is mind allied to virtue. (Harbottle 1897, p. 412) What the ancient to classical Greeks generally aspired was the truth represented by justice, virtue and beauty.

No man can be happy without virtue [Cicero] (p. 21). True happiness is centred in virtue [Seneca] (p. 21). No man can be called happy who is living a life of falsehood [Seneca] (p. 21). These Latin writers allied virtue with happiness. It was hard to find but one in thousands who shall seek, as virtue's guerdon, nought but virtue's self [Ovid] (p. 39). The first duty of man is the seeking after, and investigation of truth [Cicero] (p. 98). In stirring up tumult and strife, the worst men can do the most, but peace and quiet cannot be established without virtue [Tacitus] (p. 103). Great is truth, and all-powerful [The Vulgate] (p. 125).

Yahweh of the Old Testament shows the characteristics of anthropomorphism and displays human emotions such as compassion and hate, joy and grief, forgiveness and vengeance. God even made a mistake in making Saul king over Israel (Samuel 15:11-35).

The Old Testament repeatedly refers to the words of God 'I am a jealous God'. This utterance seems to contradict with other qualities of God such as 'God is love' or 'God is omniscient'. Jealousy is generally thought to be human deficiency and seen virtually in every human from the infant to the aged in varying fashions. In God, jealousy has a different meaning from that in mortals. Divine jealousy reveals as divine wrath and subsequently God punishes people. The greatest sin may be idolatry, which is in fact a symbolic expression of how people go after useless things. Giving up idolatry for the ancient Jews is equivalent for us modern people to give up wealth, fame, sex, good food, gambling, alcohol, drugs and even friends, families and sweethearts. Though the emotional manifestations may be expressed by the same term, the intents are different. God wants to save people by punishing them when they go after useless things in life in the fashion that people become ill if they trespass the natural limits of endurance. When we fall into illnesses such as a cold or diarrhoea, it is the nature's way of warning us that we have overworked our body or stomach. We have to remove the causes to be out of illness. God punishes us in a similar way: if we err morally we are punished until we repent and correct the root causes. The bodily sickness may come from God after all. Or the punishment of sins may come from nature. If we look at the cause and effect, God and nature may be one and the same. God or nature wishes us humans to look after our body and to be away from the worldly pursuits, leading towards justice and love among humans and ultimately towards God.

The grown-ups know that too much eating causes diarrhoea; however, the toddlers do not even understand this relationship. The toddlers know the hurt from receiving smacks. Some medical disorders come out only after years of repeated misuse of the part of the body. For example, the repeated overuse of a part of the body for many years most likely causes the aches in that part and the sufferer may not understand what causes it when it first appears. Only the reflection of the sufferer and possibly the advice of a medical doctor can reveal the cause of the problem. The bodily disorder may be comparatively easy to diagnose compared with the unhappy consequences or the curse which we can diagnose with the help of the Bible. The Bible's concern is the ethics or the way of thinking or the attitude towards life. If we choose the evil, we are sure to get bad consequences in the future; if we choose the good, we are sure to reap the good consequences in the future. Unreligious people are not aware of the relationship of the good or bad thoughts and the good or bad consequences in the future, as the toddlers are not aware of the relationship of overeating and its dire consequence. The Bible is the accumulation of vast number of experiences that the scores of authors collected over the millenniums.

The consequences, good or bad, from the way of thinking come to us without fail, whether we believe in God or not, whether we read the Bible or not, in the same way the bodily consequences, good or bad, come to us all. In both cases it is hard to know precisely what happened because of the individual differences and also some effects are too small to notice in the overall scheme of life. In this light, the moral degradation may be in fact a sickness of the brain which we acquire through the repeated wrong use. If we want to live happy and good life--though there are more than this in the religious life--we have to understand the bodily laws as well as the ethical laws and practise them earnestly and constantly. Many people eat the proper diet and do proper bodily exercises to keep fit and healthy; however, we have also to be earnest to do ethical exercises to keep ourselves ethically fit.

According to the Bible, there is a time delay between committing sins and their due punishments which are sure to come. The reason for this delay is that God gives some time for the sinner to revoke the sins and sends some warning signs before inflicting the punishment. The Wisdom of Solomon 12:10, 20, 26 refer. Also the Qur'an (30.41) says: If a person commits a sin, it normally receives a sign that what it did was not right. Juvenal, a Roman poet, wrote: But grant the wrath of Heaven be great, 'tis slow (Harbottle 1897, p. 250).

> Even an evil-doer sees good as long as evil ripens not; but when it bears fruit then he sees the evil results. Even a good person sees evil as long as good ripens not; but when it bears fruit then he sees the good results. [*The Dhammapada*, a Buddhist canon] (Narada 1993, p. 113)

There is a time delay even in the matter of health and sickness. We do not normally see any sign of good (bad) diet or proper (not enough or too much or improper) exercises in a few days and even in a few weeks; however, we know for certain that they are making their ways through our bodies and we reap the good (bad) consequences in the years to come. The following assessments are true beyond any doubt. If we abuse our body in our youth without proper medical knowledge, we get some bodily disorder in our old age. On the positive note, if we care for our bodily health in a proper way in our youth we are sure to get the benefit in our old age. We can make the same statement with confidence regarding the moral (immoral) exercises, which can be, though, hard to assess in the myriads of happenings in life. The prophets, messengers of God, see the sinful conducts of people as a whole and can predict what evils are to befall on the society. Without some delay in punishment, the prophets would not be able to forewarn the people on an impending disaster, and hence there are no such persons as prophets in a meaningful way and consequently the authors would not have written the Bible in the first place--not at least as we know it. Delay of punishment makes people feel secure in deception for a while and is the root cause of sins and subsequent evils in the society, the Good Book lectures. We normally get a warning even for a physical impediment.

One qualification to be effective prophets is the adherence to idealism, particularly to the moral codes, since idealism mostly governs the human happiness and fate, individually and collectively. The prophets can see what would befall on the society, both by virtue of time delay and by their purity of heart. It is interesting to note that Pythia, priestess of Apollo at

Delphi in the ancient to classical Greece who transmitted the oracles, was chosen from peasant women for her purity.

The prophets the world over made predictions from their intuitions (spirit) rather than from the analyses of the political, economic and social conditions (temporal) which were not available in any case. It was necessary for their intuition to be correct that their hearts were free from the impure thoughts, such as greed, anger, sexual desire and hate. We often note that when we are under these thoughts we tend to make improper speech and action in our daily life, in the same way when we are under the influence of alcohol or drugs. Just before people die, people can make sound prophecies being free from these improper thoughts. I am about to die, and this is the hour in which men are gifted with prophetic power [Aristotle] (Harbottle 1897, p. 397).

There is a Chinese saying which carries the same sense as the above disclosure:

> A man with good ears can hear what has not yet made a sound; a man with good eyes can see what has not yet taken forms. This is why a sage succeeds in all he does. (Chien 1979, p. 323)

The biblical teachings also tell us the above assertion that idealism mostly governs the fate of human beings. There were possibly hundreds of prophets in the Levant at any time, each preaching his or her predictions: only the careful readers can make this out. In fact the mass of sayings from so many prophets must have confused people. The Bible tells the criteria by which people can judge: if what the prophets say come true in the future, they lived according to the precepts of God, and acceptable to God and genuine. The authors of the Bible carried out the foolproof method by choosing only the sayings of the prophets whose words came true at the later date hence its contents mostly match with the facts we know today.

Animals do not philosophise about life and death. They go on living as best they can until death grips them in some way or another. In fact they have no fear of death until they are about to die: they are not capable of contemplating of dying beforehand. Only the humans (savages and civilised persons) can be afraid to die while they are not in danger of immediate peril. The fear of death must have driven the human beings to wish for eternal life and, in conjunction, for the presence of an omnipotent being. This is another reason why people have cherished the concept of Almighty God. In this light people with the idea of God are not animals.

Certain individuals in a tribe in the primitive world were recognised as having special power to communicate with nature, gods or God, and acted as messengers or intermediaries. They were variously called mediums, seers, prophets and shamans as the case may be. It seems that generally the transference of the messages became the nucleus of governorship. The messengers and rulers were held in high esteem and must have done their best to keep deity in awe in turn. It is not hard to guess that the rulers if they were not the messengers must have colluded with these individuals who professed to have special skill to communicate with higher being, and used them as their mouth piece. In this sense, deity was a useful tool for the messengers and the rulers.

'This association between Shamanism and political hierarchy reached its peak with the Shang and Zhou (Chou) rulers of the Bronze Age, whose rule was backed on their claim to communicate with divine authority.' (Murowchik 1994, p. 55) During the Zhou era in China, the king bore the title 'Son of Heaven' and had the unique right to make sacrifices to Heaven at the capital. The Son of Heaven had the power of life or death over all his subjects under heaven, who accepted the authority without question. In historical China rulers often acted as messengers as well.

To communicate with gods or to atone for the calamity, many peoples the world over sacrificed humans or animals. The human sacrifices are well documented for Semitic,

Chinese and Inca peoples. For example, Moloch is a god of Ammonites and children were offered to it as sacrifices. In the eminent world religions, this concept was superseded and the ethical life is supposed to be favourable to get the attention of gods. Still we can see some common threads running, that is, people do something for gods to get their attention.

Moses, as the Bible narrates, was both a medium and a ruler, thus commanded a tremendous authority among the Israelites during the Exodus. Before and during the age of Moses, in the traditional Chinese society and probably in many other early civilisations, the division of labour between the intermediary and the ruler did not exist. The Jews were fighting for sheer survival during the journey from Egypt to the Levant and the dual authority in one person was a necessity, a matter of life or death. Isaiah, Jeremiah and even Jesus Christ were not rulers of the temporal world but remained God's intermediaries criticising the people in the temporal world. There was some evidence to suggest that Christ tried to seize temporal power, when he was arrested and eventually crucified. The era of dual authority was clearly over in his time in Judaea at least.

Many historical records in China refer to Tian (Heaven); however, they also sometimes mentions a supreme celestial god, Di (Lord) or Shang-di (The Lord on High). The Bronze Age when the above nominations first appeared roughly corresponds to the Shang dynasty (c. 1751-1028 BC).

> Ti [Di] commands the cosmic rhythms and natural phenomena (rain, wind, drought, etc.); he grants the king victory and insures the abundance of crops, or brings on disasters and sends sickness and death (Eliade 1982, p. 7).
>
> Ti is found to be distant and less active than the ancestors of the royal lineage and he is offered fewer sacrifices. But he alone is involved in matters of fecundity (rain) and war, the sovereign’s two preoccupations. (p. 7)
>
> Ti is the Supreme Being, and all the other gods and the royal ancestors are subordinate to him. Only the king’s ancestors are able to intercede with Ti, and only the king communicates with his ancestors. The above set-up strengthens the authority of the king. (p. 3)

At the beginning of the Zhou dynasty the celestial god Tian (T’ien) or Shang-di (Shang-ti) shows the characteristics of an anthropomorphic and perfect god. Later Tian loses religious nature and becomes the principle of cosmic order, the warrant of moral law; in other words, Tian comes close to the concept of Heaven of the Western world. (p. 10)

Section 2 Various Religions

Religions as used in this series of books contain idealism; the main components of idealism in turn contain morals (or virtues and ethics), which is practically the same as "Love thy neighbour'. However, the core theories of Buddhism and Christianity have very little to do with idealism though I present that they are built on idealism. Hence readers may have some difficulty in understanding the arguments to follow in this respect.

It is a general rule that the people compiled great arts when they formed a nation from chaos, or the nation came out triumphantly from the momentous events to determine its destiny such as effective political or religious reforms, or the end of the long lasting wars, or victory over the fearful enemy who threatened to exterminate the nation. In all cases the bulk of the population feel relief that the past sufferings were over and look forward to the bright future. Literature, a form of arts, is an expression of joy and happiness and takes various forms such as dramas (comics or tragedies), poetry and essays.

The Elizabethan era (1558-1603) with its magnificent flowering of literature typifies the statements in the last paragraph, though the contemporary Puritans criticised Queen Elizabeth I (1533-1603) for the promotion of dramas similarly Buddhism condemns musical or literary productions which do not promote spiritual wellbeing. We can see the parallel today of the parents not wanting some books and movies for their children. The English people rejoiced when the English crown passed to Elizabeth when Bloody Mary died in 1558 after 5 years of reign. Mary married Prince Philip (future King Philip II) of Spain one year after becoming English queen. The marriage was extremely unpopular among the English because many English people viewed Spain as the greatest enemy nation, and the English Parliament refused to crown him. She wanted to establish Catholic rule in England and persecuted Protestants and executed hundreds of heretics. She was a devout Roman Catholic and was determined to force England back to the Catholic faith. The allegation stuck with her that her birth was illegitimate being born from the incestuous relation when Henry divorced Catherine with papal condemnation. Her mother Catherine was a Catholic and of Spanish blood, though a label of a bastard did not prevent Mary becoming an English queen.

English Parliament passed the Act of Supremacy and the Act of Uniformity both in 1559, and confirmed Elizabeth as the Supreme Governor of the Church of England as well as independence of the church from Rome. Thus, Queen Elizabeth made the Church of England the state religion; her power base was in Protestantism, or if more narrowly expressed, in Anglicanism. However she guaranteed the freedom of worship for Catholics in England. Thus she brought an end to the general unrest in England ending the religious wars by her compromise of the middle path. Her judgement was acute and right. In fact only after the Catholics and Protestants realised that they could not win over the other side through Thirty Years' of War (1618-48) the compromise and peace prevailed in continental Europe after a century of Elizabeth's compromise; in France peace prevailed after half a century of Elizabeth's compromise. Many historians emphasise her contribution to ushering in the era of the great literature; however, the earlier statement of this section makes light of her personal role though she was the one who brought the political and religious stability in England. Also her navy defeated the Spanish Armada (1588) sent by King Philip II. Spain was the most powerful nation in Europe at the time and the English were fearful of Spain and its powerful armada. The defeat of the armada constituted the historic importance. Some people say there was a great deal of lucks involved in the victory against the armada; among which was the fact that a fierce storm destroyed many of the Spanish ships. I mentioned only a few of her achievements. It was the results that were important in these events as in many other events, which showed up as the joyous feeling of the English people and subsequent flowering of literature. The foundation of the British Empire was laid during her era. The British Empire is said to have started during the reign of Queen Elizabeth I and ended during the reign of Queen Elizabeth II.

Literature as used above is a form of arts, whereas religious literature is an expression of religion. I esteem both, together with idealism, are the survival means of the humans.

The birth of religion is diametrically different from the production of literature. Religions came out among the primitive peoples the world over when they felt powerless about such as fear of death, the overwhelming natural forces, dreadful enemies, and deadly diseases, and they had to pray asking for help from the higher order. Also the great religions were born when the well-ordered societies went through disintegration and the people agonised to the extreme. People tormented themselves thinking why a certain calamity struck them personally or socially. The people naturally have to devise the means by which they can escape the mental pains. Unless people suffer there is no reason to develop religion.

Writing system was developed in Greece in about 1000 BC and by c. 720 BC the Greeks fully established their alphabets. The works of the poets, Homer (c. 800 BC) and Hesiod (8th century BC), and also those of three tragic dramatists, Aeschylus, Sophocles and Euripides are all literature. The first two poets of the formative era of the Greek city-states set the foundation of the Greek culture. The crucial victories, at Marathon (490 BC) and Salamis (480 BC) against the Persians, took place during the life times of the above three dramatists; and their works reflected the triumphant and proud era. The Greeks from the ancient to classical eras were characterised with harmony and creative genius in diverse fields. They developed not only distinct arts such as literature above mentioned, but also sculpture and architecture, and made major contributions to history, science, psychology, political thinking represented by democracy and so on.

It is rather surprising that the Greeks with a small population exhibited their talents in such wide ranging subjects. The reasons can only be guessed. One reason may be a long time of cultural ascendancy, that is, from the establishment of alphabets c. 720 BC to the outbreak of the Peloponnesian War in 431 BC. Also the Greeks conducted land and sea trade extensively with the peoples with high cultures and their social fabric made them learn and get the inspiration for higher wisdom. Furthermore, the Greek cities were ever in competition to excel each other to develop their cultures.

Socrates, Plato and Aristotle presented their solutions to the sufferings coming from the collapse of polis society whose pinnacle is said to be during the reign of Pericles (495-429 BC). He was elected to power in Athens about 460 BC and strengthened Athenian democracy. The golden age of the Greeks is said to have come to an end in 431 BC, at the outbreak of the Peloponnesian War. He conducted the Peloponnesian War successfully until his death.

Socrates, Plato and Aristotle focused their attention on idealism and religion, though Aristotle further made inquiries into wide spectrum of studies and his scientific investigation was noteworthy. Idealism, one of the survival strategies of the humans, crystallises into religion. Though I present them separately in this series of books, the distinction between them is hard to make and hazy. Socrates (469-399 BC) himself witnessed the entire length of Peloponnesian War (431-404 BC) and the passing of the golden age of Athens.

I refer to how Confucianism, Daoism and Legalism were developed in China when she was going through the Warring States period (475-221 BC) in Section 1, Chapter 2, Book One.

Around 1700 BC, the Indus Valley civilisation by the Dravidians started to break up possibly as the result of the changed pattern of the Indus River and a consequent series of floods. The period was coincided with the invasions of the Indo-Europeans who called themselves the Aryans with the sense of racial superiority over the native Dravidians. Subsequently the Indo-Europeans settled in the plain of the Ganges River by 1000 BC. The plain was fertile, and the spread of iron tools increased the agricultural productivity though the first use of iron tools in India dates back to 1800 BC. The economy in these regions always centred around cow raising, which resulted in esteeming cows as sacred, that is, very important. These two cultures interacted and it is said that yoga and meditation practised by Hinduism originated in the Indus Valley culture (Dravidian). The social turmoil and the mixing of the two races created fears among the Hindus (the Indo-Europeans) and led to the creation of Brahmanism and later Hinduism. Hinduism thus born has a racial element and the Hindus thought that the caste system integrating classism and racism was a divine order. The Indo-Europeans from Central Asia before emigration had the three class system ingrained in their society. In the sixth and fifth centuries BC, the centre of power in India shifted from the Indus, the seat of the earlier civilisation, to the Ganges plain. Politically the period was of continuous strife, and the political turmoil centred on the control of the Ganges River. Magadha Kingdom became victorious, becoming the nucleus of several kingdoms from the 6th century BC to the AD 8th century. Gautama Siddhartha was born in one of the states in 563 BC: his father was a ruler of a poor Indian tribe, the Sakyas. Gautama was in fact a reformist of Hinduism. The modern scholars established only bare facts of the historical Buddha and could not prove the authenticity of many of the legendary accounts of his life. I can make the similar statements about Jesus Christ who appeared half millennium later and tried to reform Judaism.

The birth of Judaism is quite different from the birth of religion and idealism above mentioned. Judaism and its derivatives, Christianity and Islam, may be the only religion with the strong focus on the Almighty and God among the major religious thoughts of the present world, which suggests that we must seek a distinct reason for the formation of Judaism.

In the second place the formation of the Hebrew Bible took much longer than the time limitations of religion and idealism which as a rule came forth during decaying years of the well-ordered society covering only a few generations, again suggesting different causes for the origination of the Hebrew Bible. All the major religions have the roots at the formation of the race or nation. The scores of the Jewish authors, who lived apart stretching for over one millennium, wrote the above book, as representing Judaism, though the stories written about the Jewish people go much longer than that. Though the creative period of Mesopotamia ended around 1500 BC, the Jewish genius as exemplified in the creation of the Hebrew Bible began long before 1500 BC and ended long after. There was a cultural unity in the eastern Mediterranean before the Indo-European invasion of 1500-1100 BC. Generally the Hebrew Bible is thought to be the canon of Judaism, and this Bible is somewhat different from the Old Testament, a part of the Christian Bible.

When people come under serious threats such as political and racial causes some survival means come forward strongly. Also when people come out to joyous social environment some survival means come forward strongly. The plants and animals now extant have devised the means of survival. The plants and animals extinct could not devise the means of survival and perished.

Every religion and every idealism tackle the agony of people mirroring its unique social problems. Formation of religion and idealism was generally thought to be the product of the disintegration of the well-ordered society. Buddhism, Confucianism and Greek philosophy do not deviate from this observation. However, in the case of the Jewish religion we can locate the problems in the Jews' evil conducts, and the consequent social unrest and pogroms. Pogroms existed as long as the Jewish people existed and were the relentless attacks on the existence of the Jews and the Jewish state. Hence the sufferings by the Jews were not only political or social but racial. The deep sufferings felt by the Jews led to the total commitment to the Almighty, the intelligent insights into human natures and societies, and adoption of defensive racism. Buddhist doctrines incidentally refer to god and do not try to delve into human natures and societies, and keep absolute silence on politics and racism. Both religions totally ignore the economic aspect of the human activities.

The Jews went through sufferings coming from both the social turmoil and pogroms since their appearance on earth and also had a joy coming from the formation of the Jewish state, and the Old Testament is a religious book as well as literature. The Old Testament is the survival guide and at the same time the expression of gladness in seeing the re-formation of the new state following the Exodus. One story goes that the Old Testament was written down just after the Jewish state was formed, that is, in the reigns of King David and King Solomon. The sufferings over one millennium overpower the joyful feeling of a brief period, and the Old Testament as a whole is a religious book. Without the compilation of the Old Testament it is hard for us to imagine that the Jews have survived the persecutions through millenniums. The religions, as symbols, are the most powerful of the social cohesions. The pogroms have been the curse for the Jews all through their existence. The term pogrom denotes the attacks on the Jews for being Jew. The conquest of the Jews by a foreign nation as the canon describes is also an abomination, no different from pogroms if we look at the agony of the Jewish people.

'Introduction to Series' in Book One describes how Judaism metamorphosed into Christianity and further these two religions metamorphosed into Islam. The political reasons necessitated both metamorphoses; however, the authors of the latter two creeds carefully preserved the fundamentals of Judaism leaving out the racial element.

Idealism crystallises into religion and it is hard to make distinctions between the two in practice. Religion deals with the absolute, the ultimate, gods, God or Heaven. I have come to believe that once religion was firmly established it has very little to do with idealism or how people should conduct themselves in relation to the fellow human beings. Particularly Christianity and Buddhism make the distinction clear as shown in their systematic creed. I am to highlight the distinction in chapters 2 and 3 respectively.

Idealism and materialism may achieve the happiness of the individuals, the establishment of an empire and the increase of population. However, these resultant effects have very little to do with religion.

It is possible to establish religion not going through idealism and there are other means to reach to the absolute, the ultimate. These other means do not involve the disintegration of the ordered society or the racial persecution; however, they all involve the fears and sufferings of people. Without fears and sufferings people did not have any need to rely on idealism and religion.

Idealism is on the human dimensions and religion is on the higher plane. For example: Mind Only (or Emptiness) of Buddhism and love of God of Judaism leave behind the human affairs utterly and deny even the concept of 'Love thy neighbour'.

Originally people sought religion to escape sufferings but this does not explain what religion is. People went beyond what they set out and sought religion for its own sake or for truth, in the process enduring unspeakable sufferings. We can see the similar human traits in the establishment of the harems through the course of the human history. The kings set up the harems for their enjoyment; however, the eunuchs in the harems often murdered the kings in their hot pursuit of the gains. I describe this aspect of human behaviours in conjunction with Egypt and China in Section 7 Harem, Chapter 1, Book Five *The Sexual Laws.*

It seems that unimpressive arts and unimpressive religion do not follow the above general rule, and came forth not involving any unification or disintegration of the society or the persecution of the people or the deep fear of their surrounding world. It is a logical statement that mundane joy and mundane suffering produce only mundane arts and mundane religion. Also there must be other factors operating besides the above causes in the society for the formation of great arts and great religion, which only the extreme joy for the former and the deep suffering for the latter, each as a society as a whole, are capable of producing. The fears and sufferings of the Jews were very deep and continuous, which produced deep insight into the human natures and correspondingly unique and marvellous religion.

The foregoing observations are for the community as a whole. It may happen that an individual goes through joy and suffering to the extreme not reflecting those in the society. However, that person is unlikely to produce great works. History has shown it is the norm that a large number of people must contribute such that an eminent individual could build great works utilising these contributions: If there are no works by a large number of people even a genius cannot create anything spectacular.

This corresponds to the consequence of the evil conducts of the community as a whole. The Bible says that the evil society has the evil consequence waiting without fail, though a small number of people within the community may go against the tide and live according to the religious faiths.

Observing both cases involving extreme joy and extreme suffering for the community as a whole, we can give the credence to the conviction of Plato that humans are social beings and more than individual existence.

Major religious thoughts in China, Greece and India were formulated in the early classical era, that is, just after 500 BC. Judaism, Christianity and Islam took shape on the different time frame. After the establishment of these religious thoughts and religions, when the peoples suffered as the result of the social turmoil the peoples relied on them to relieve their mental agony instead of devising new religions.

The foregoing observations match with the behaviours of the general public today. When people are doing well in their life they go for arts, and when they are suffering they go for religion; provided they do not go after low pleasures such as drugs, alcohol and the like. Today people have a large number of choices in the selection of arts and religions.

Every person and every culture looked at the life and the world differently and expressed them accordingly. Montaigne wrote:

> Some say that our good lies in virtue, others in sensual pleasure, others in conforming to nature; one man in knowledge, one in having no pain, one in not letting ourselves be carried away by appearances (Montaigne 1965, p. 435).

So it is not surprising that there are many ways of expressing the religious thinking in the world: One Supreme God as in Judaism, Christianity and Islam; the multitudes of gods as in the ancient Greek religion; Heaven as in Confucianism; and the Law as in Buddhism.

If we look at the lives of human races throughout history, we at once notice that they all had a concept of divinity represented in some way or another. We can make the same statement about the primitive tribes still existing today. All peoples through human history: however powerful or weak; advanced or primitive; surrounded or isolated, had a notion of divinity integrated into the community and hence into the thinking process of the individuals.

We can variously express the concept of divinity as deity, providence, supernatural, god or gods. They certainly have different meanings to different peoples, but as readers will see in this book, I find that the differences are only the way they are expressed and are no different in substance as I stress in this series of books. However, as far as the core theories of

Buddhism and Christianity are concerned, they are doctrinally well developed and what they assert is different from the others and each other.

Every people expressed the idea of deity or divinity in a way to mirror its environments. Mountain people naturally must have associated deity with what they see around them--rocks, trees and mountains and so on. Sea faring or desert people must have represented deity in relation to the sea, the desert, the sun, the moon and the stars. Understandably all these peoples tried to explain the mysteries of life in terms of will of deity in the absence of scientific knowledge.

Leviathan (1651) by Thomas Hobbes unfolds:

> And for that part of religion which consisteth in opinions concerning the nature of powers invisible, there is almost nothing that has a name that has not been esteemed amongst the Gentiles, in one place or another, a god or devil; or by their poets feigned to be animated, inhabited, or possessed by some spirits or other. The unformed matter of the world was a god by the name of Chaos. The heaven, the ocean, the planets, the fire, the earth, the winds were so many gods. (Hutchins 1952, p. 81)

The ancient people carried out the rituals venerating the various gods, but that does not mean people believed in what they did. Similarly people bring out Santa Clause during Christmas in the Christian world today, but that does not follow people believe in him. Both rituals are custom, culture and way of life and people carry out what they think proper.

Apart from Confucianism, Buddhism and Daoism (Taoism), there were cults at many levels of Chinese society. The imperial cult took the form of a series of grand ceremonies that were performed to inaugurate the seasons, ensure good harvests, honour Heaven and Earth, placate the appropriate deities and make ancestor worship. The people at the other levels of the social strata also conducted the similar worship matching their means. (Harris 1999, p. 113)

Nature deities such as river, mountain and weather spirits were venerated in China. In Vedic verses, speech, consciousness, life, water, wind and fire symbolised as deities in India. In later Mazdaism, fire is identified with Holy Spirit: it together with the sun is associated with Ahura Mazda. The sun is the visible form of Lord. Truth is likewise associated with light. (Eliade 1978, p. 322) Zarathustra, the Avestan name for the Persian prophet Zoroaster, is obsessed with the punishment of the wicked, and the rewarding of the virtuous. He exclaimed:

> What penalty is provided for him who procures empire for the evil doer? When shall I learn if you have power, O Wise One (Mazda) with justice, over each of those who threaten me with destruction? (p. 306)

Asshur (Assur) is the highest god among the Pantheon in Assyria. Assyria was named after him.

> Its inhabitants are 'his servants,' or 'his people;' its troops, 'the armies of the God Asshur [Assur];' its enemies, 'the enemies of Asshur.' The kings stand connected with him in respect of almost everything which they do. He places them upon the throne, firmly establishes them in the government, lengthens the years of their reigns, preserves their power, protects their forts and armies, directs their expeditions, gives them victory in the day of battle, makes their name celebrated, multiplies their offspring greatly, and the like. The divine figures were presented to inspire awe and reverence to the spectators. (Sheowring & Thies 1982, p. 12)

China and India produced their defining literature as art in their history when people in these countries felt that they achieved their desired political or social status.

Under the heading of the regions I am to present only the main religious thinking in the following text. Obviously the foregoing regions of the world contained a huge number of religious thoughts, presentation of which obscure the thrust of the argument rather than help.

India
Sir John Hubert Marshall (1876-1958), a British archaeologist, first identified the Indus civilisation (pre-Aryan) with its sophisticated material culture, and proceeded with the excavations at Harappa (1921) and Mohenjo-daro (1922). The material clues suggest that these cultures were highly religious, flourishing from 2500 to 1750 BC. (Koller 1985, p. 20) They were literate civilisation. Though the written language has not been deciphered it is classed to be Dravidian.

'The Aryans had begun their advance into north-western India at the beginning of the second millennium BC: four or five centuries later they occupied the region of the Seven Rivers, that is, the basin of the Upper Indus, the Punjab.' (Eliade 1978, p. 195) The Aryans referred are the Indo-Iranians who are members of the Indo-European families. The Indo-Iranians originally came from north of modern Afghanistan, now known as Turkistan where the Iranian languages are still spoken.

Sanskrit language, of which the Vedas were the oldest surviving expression, became the primary vehicle of Indian thought. Numerous Middle Indo-Aryan languages, called the Prakrit, evolved from Sanskrit and its dialects.

Sanskrit became widespread in the Indian continent by the beginning of the fifth century BC except in the south where Dravidian language was spoken. The epic poems of *Mahabharata* and *Ramayana* are the famous Sanskrit literature produced at around this era. (Ostler 2006, p. 176) Both are important Hindu sacred writings, and the latter contains the Bhagavad-Gita, in which the god Krishna discusses the nature and meaning of existence.

The expansion of Brahmanism and, some century later, of Hinduism followed closely on the Aryanisation of the sub-continent (Eliade 1982, p. 44). The Vedic texts present Varuna as sovereign god: he reigns over the world, the gods and men. He is visible everywhere, omniscient and infallible. Varuna re-establishes the order damaged by sin, error or ignorance. The sinner hopes for absolution through sacrifices.

The Vedic hymns and the Brahmanic treatise were made for the elite class of the aristocrats and priests, and they did not include the popular religious life of the Aryan society.

Yogin knew experimentally from the earliest times that there is always a connection between respiration and the mental state. By controlling respiration yogins tried to create unified state of consciousness. Yoga Sutra goes: By concentrating on the subconscious residues, one knows his former lives; By meditating one can assimilate and possess its contents; By renouncing some pleasures, one can obtain true happiness far exceeding the pleasures one renounces. (pp. 63, 68) The yogins seek the truth by self-discipline, separating the good from the bad.

'Liberation from suffering is the goal of all Indian philosophies and techniques of meditation. No knowledge has any value if it does not pursue the salvation of man. Except for that [i.e., except for the Eternal that resides in the Self], nothing is worth knowing.' The Upanishads state that 'suffering, which defines the human condition, is the result of unknowing'. (pp. 46, 48) This reminds us of the famous Socrates' teaching. In contrast with the above view, Plato believed that the highest truth was the goodness and the philosophers must devote themselves with the pursuit of the good. In India there is no distinction between religion and philosophy.

A core belief of Hinduism may be that human beings are tied to a cycle of death and rebirth, known as the samsara. They can escape this unfortunate process through transmigration of the soul into union with Brahman, the eternal ideal behind all existence. Release may be sought through learning asceticism or devotion. However, the Hindus believe that the caste system is a part of the divine social order and they did not alter this conviction when political dominance passed to the Muslim Mughals and to the alien British. (Davison 1993, p. 33) Buddhism rejected the caste system.

Indian philosophy generally encompasses the following formula:

existence = suffering

Leibniz attempted to show how a perfect and all powerful God created a world full of sufferings and evils.

Its cause is ignorance comparable with sleep, dream, intoxication and captivity. The awakening or enlightenment can remove all the causes of suffering. One becomes delivered from suffering by acquiring knowledge. Three characteristics of Brahmanism are:

Vedanta (interpretations of sacred texts)
Samkhya (philosophy)
Yoga

Hinduism incorporated the Vedic tradition of effectiveness of mantras uttered, even though the utterers do not understand their meanings: contact with the sacred words was thought to be in contact with the gods (Kung et al. 1986, p. 149). This compares with the observation that many people enjoy songs, even though they don't understand their meanings. However, mantras and songs may be diametrically opposed in their purposes in that the former teaches escape from suffering and the latter is for pleasure only.

Vedic tradition, that is, the four sacred writings of Hinduism, was composed between 1500 and 700 BC:

Rig-Veda, the oldest and principal of Vedas, consists of a collection of hymns.
Yajur-Veda records all sayings to be used while performing sacrifices.
Sama-Veda contains rituals for sacrifices.
Atharva-Veda consists of priestly spells and incantations.

With the rise of Hinduism, the Buddhist faith by the eighth century had become an empty shell of a religion in India. The Buddha's disciples did not emphasise that the Buddha built his beliefs from Hinduism, which may be one reason why the Indians or Hindus rejected his teachings. Hinduism tended to absorb rather than attack alien religions and did exactly that with Buddhism. Indian Buddhism retained its separate religious identity only in the fringes of the Indian world--in the lands of Sri Lanka, Burma and Tibet. (The Editors of Time-Life Books 1988, p. 93)

A monk introduced Buddhism into Tibet in the second half of the 8th century, and it was firmly established there in the 11th century. These facts are surprising in that Tibet was only 200 miles from where the Buddha lived. Dalai Lama, head of Tibetan Buddhism, served as the political and religious leader of Tibet from the 1600s to 1959, when the 14th Dalai Lama escaped to India in the wake of Chinese invasion of Tibet.

In India around the ninth century, a fresh approach appeared in the Vedic tradition of four Vedas tentatively at first. The emphasis of offering sacrifices to the gods diminished, and the new approach of philosophy came forward, and the Brahmana text and Upanishads articulated it. This also gave rise to the concept of monistic thought replacing polytheism. (Kung et al. 1986, p. 150) The Bramanas and Upanishads were important later additions to the Vedas. The former explains the significance of rites and the latter is highly speculative works searching for unity in existence. Both gave rise to the Indian philosophy.

Greece

The myth that the beginning was like a paradise for humans until they committed sins is widespread: for example, the biblical story of Adam and Eve, and the Greek mythology as narrated by Hesiod in *Works and Days*. Theocritus expressed this view when he read a poem, ''T was then the golden age of human kind, those far-off days when loved ones love returned' (Harbottle 1897, p. 387).

Ancient to classical Greeks conceived a group of gods, each having his or her sphere of influence. The gods are passionately concerned with human affairs and use their power to assist favourites and to harm enemies (Cotterell 1993, p. 16). All the gods had capriciousness of human beings, though they were thought to be immortal. According to the Greek mythology, the gods often acted from vengeance, jealousy and even spite. They interfered with human affairs at will, which undoubtedly came from the fact that unforeseen events interrupt our human life and as a consequence the life takes unpredictable course. The ancient to classical Greeks talked that the gods lived in Mount Olympus. This legend itself suggests that they were human-like in contrast with the Jewish God who was omnipresent.

Zeus recognised the supremacy of justice and in the *Iliad* Zeus was the protector of justice. Justice is only the concrete manifestation, in the human society, of the universal order, in other words, of the Divine Law, the chief of which is 'Love thy neighbour'. Hesiod declared that Zeus bestowed justice on men so that they would not behave like wild beasts. The first duty of men is to be just and to show honours to the gods, especially offering them sacrifices. The extreme of injustice is when what is unjust is held to be just [Plato] (Montaigne 1965, p. 798). Truth appears in the form of justice and beauty. They are not necessarily omnipresent; they can be trampled down and may not be found for a while. Without justice beauty cannot make any sense. Justice and beauty are gods (truth). Thus Pythagoras said, 'Concealing the truth is like burying gold' (Harbottle 1897, p. 493).

Beauty is a powerful and advantageous quality. The ancient to classical Greeks thought that good things in life may be health, beauty and riches. In Greek language the same word embraces the beautiful and the good. Socrates called it 'a short tyranny' and Plato, 'the privilege of nature'. (Montaigne 1965, p. 810)

> In short, the gods do not strike men without reason, as long as the mortals do not go beyond the limits prescribed by their own mode of existence. But it is difficult not to go the imposed limits, for man's ideal is excellence. Now, excessive excellence runs the risk of arousing inordinate pride and insolence. ... insolence brings on a temporary madness, which blinds the victim and leads him to disaster. (Eliade 1978, p. 261)
>
> Three fundamental theses of Socrates are so closely related as to form scarcely separable parts of a single whole. They are: virtue is knowledge; its converse, that wrongdoing can only be due to ignorance and must therefore be considered involuntary; and care of the soul as the primary condition of living well. (Guthrie 1969, p. 450)
>
> So in life, we cannot acquire an art of self-improvement unless we first understand what we ourselves are. Our first duty, therefore, is to obey the Delphic command, 'Know thyself'. For once we know ourselves, we may learn how to care for ourselves, but otherwise we never shall. (p. 471)

> A humble knowledge of thyself is a surer way to God than a deep search after learning; yet learning is not to be blamed, nor the mere knowledge of anything

> whatsoever to be disliked, it being good in itself and ordained by God; but a good conscience and a virtuous life are always to be preferred before it (Thomas a Kempis 1980, p. 29).
>
> Who has a fiercer struggle than he who strives to conquer himself? Yet this must be our chief concern—conquer self, and by daily growing stronger to advance in holiness. (Thomas A Kempis 1952, p. 30)

Einstein wrote that imagination is more important than knowledge. He was referring to the different sphere of human activities. He was talking about his experience in the field of scientific research. When the interviewers interview the applicants to fill the vacancies, they look for knowledge and experience once they establish the necessary educational, trade or professional, qualifications. At present people don't know how to assess the imagination of the applicants hence the interviewers disregard this point. My experience shows that people with good imagination are more useful for the firm than the people who bring only the theories and experience. Reason goes against the creative work at the initial stage (Freud 1982, p. 103). Certainly this idea will raise a criticism in that granted my assessment may be correct they cannot keep the people who do not reach a certain level of theoretical and practical competency.

Socrates served as a hoplite on occasions in the Peloponnesian War. He played virtually no part in politics. He was charged with corrupting the youths and neglecting the gods whom the city worshiped. He said:

> The young should get instructions; grown men should practice doing good; and old men should withdraw from all civil and military occupations and live at their own discretion, without being tied down to any fixed office (Montaigne 1965, p. 178).

Socrates was the chief inspiration of the Plato's life. '... none of the political proposals in *The Republic* [by Plato] are seriously meant; which, at least in the sense that his purpose was to shed further light on human nature and moral principles, and he had no intention of bringing his imagined state into existence ....' (Guthrie 1975, p. 464)

Delphic oracles more often than not spoke in riddles, and people had to work out what was the true meaning from what was the obvious statement. Aristotle referred to a Delphic sword, a two-edged sword, in reference to the ambiguities of the Delphic oracles.

> When his, i.e., Socrates', friend Cherephon consulted the Pythia to find out whether there was anyone in the world wiser than Socrates the oracle replied that no such man existed (Flaceliere 1965, p. 59).

The Delphic Maxims, 147 aphorisms in all, were inscribed in the temple of Delphi, and said to be from the lips of Apollo. Delphi's maxim 'Nothing in Excess' is a universal truth which many philosophers the world over preached as middle path, and it is true to us today as was true to the ancient to classical Greeks. Whoever has not heeded to the significance of the above saying has paid dear to their detriment. Though some maxims are foreign to us; some, as below, are still relevant to us:

Know thyself.
Aid friends.
Watch out for your enemies.
Control yourself.

Shun injustice.
Know what you have learned.
Be yourself.
Cling to disciplines.
Be impartial.
Be a seeker of wisdom.
Refrain the tongue.
Keep yourself from insolence.
Acquire wealth justly.

Socrates highly esteemed divination, particularly the oracle of Delphi. The Delphic inscription 'Know thyself' was thought to be the essence of virtue and was the heart of Socrates' teaching. Thales also promulgated this doctrine (Harbottle 1897, p. 346). Socrates used to say that the principal function of wisdom was to distinguish the good from the bad (Montaigne 1965, p. 245). Archytas said, 'Happiness lies not in the possession but in the practice of virtue' (Harbottle 1897, p. 450).

Plato also showed reverence for Pythian Apollo.

Since the outbreak of the Persian Wars, the Delphic oracles ceased to be impartial or at least the Greeks thought so. The Pythia was accused that she sided with the Persians at the time of the Xerxes' invasion, the Spartans during the Peloponnesian War, and again Philip of Macedonia.

The Delphic oracles held sway in the Greek world for more than a millennium, from 800 BC or earlier till AD 381 when the Romans destroyed the site.

Our sources of information on Socrates are practically four: Aristophanes, Xenophon, Plato, Aristotle.

> There is plenty of evidence that as a young man Socrates was an enthusiast for natural science of his time, but later he condemned it for irrelevance to human problems and its neglect of final causes. It was barren and did not care for the souls. (Guthrie 1969, p. 407)

Politics did not interest Socrates. The above change on the part of Socrates, some people claim, brought the change in Athenian interest from natural science to the problems of human life.

> He lived and spoke according to certain principles, which brought him into conflict, now with the dictatorial Thirty and again with the restored democracy, and set him apart from all political ambitions (p. 413).
>
> Socrates gave up science for ethics, the study of nature for the pursuit of practical principles. But, perhaps because of his early scientific studies, he insisted that ethics itself was a field of exact knowledge calling for the application of rigorous scientific method. (p. 424)
>
> So long as any belief in an anthropomorphic polytheism survives, gods will be thought of as capricious beings, whose favour will depend on our fulfilling their wishes, and the main part of religious duty will consist in the difficult task of discovering what they want in order to give it to them--a kind of commercial transaction, as Socrates calls it (Guthrie 1975, p. 110).

Mediums, Pythias or prophets passed the messages in the form of oracles and prophecies; they were thought to be from divinity, though they were undoubtedly human creations. The preferred terms in the Bible are prophets, seers or the servants of God; in the Qur'an (Koran), messenger of God, emphasising that the messenger does not contribute apart from what God passes to him.

Pythia pronounced the oracles of Apollo, a Greek deity; the god of light, healing, music, poetry, prophecy and so forth. Pythia led the life of a recluse and lived a life of complete chaste and purity. Delphi was the site of temple of Apollo. When Pythia was prophesying she was in a state of frenzy; self-hypnotism or auto-suggestion may have caused her madness.

Herodotus above all and also Plutarch preserved many of the Delphic oracles and inscriptional evidence. The prestige of the Delphic oracles was great at least up to the Persian Wars. The divination in the form of the Delphic oracles reached its peak in the sixth century BC, and up to the fourth century BC the people of Athens as a whole believed in the oracles. Up to the Persian Wars the authority of the oracles seems to have been practically unchallenged. (Flaceliere 1965, pp. 42-3, 50-1, 53, 55, 57)

Were the gods only the entertainment in the same way as we regard the movies and talk about them? Did the Greeks regard the words of the oracles as binding as the laws of a democratic society? Certainly the oracles in Greek plays come out true in the end as the Shakespearean tragedies do. But that does not answer my question because of the necessity of being so from the setup of the play: readers would find the plot ridiculous if the prophecy does not fulfil itself in the unfolding of the story. The play writers had to organise the fulfilment of the prophecy in such a way to give the maximum effect. It seems that before the 4th century BC the oracles in the Greek world were taken seriously overriding the other economic and political considerations, which were not fully developed in the earlier centuries in any case. 'The decision to send out colonists and where to send them, the right behaviour in a national emergency, even legal and constitutional question, were all sometimes determined by oracle.' For example, the oracle of Delphi was guidance on the sites when the Greek city planned the colonisation. However, it seems that the practical grounds of survival decided the final choice of the colonising site. Delphi where the oracles of Apollo were consulted was considered to be the most prestigious. The oracles of the Olympia and Delos also had substantial influence on the Greeks. (Levi 1980, p. 73)

Middle East (Judaism-Christianity-Islam)

Refer to 'Introduction to Series', Book One *Idealism and Materialism*, for the social, political and racial reasons why these strands of religion came into being.

The ancient Jews had a rigid system of religious doctrines as is obvious from reading the Old Testament. Undoubtedly many Jews took religion at its face value and considered it crucial to the survival of their race. The deep devotion of the ancient Jews passed to the modern Jews and also to the Christians and the Muslims alike. This series of religion emphasises one supreme God who is omniscient and omnipotent. The believers of these religions are to follow their holy books without questioning. It is significant that all these and even Nestorian Christianity originated in the Middle East—encompassing so-called the Cradle of Civilisation. The seriousness towards religion characterises this series of faith and all these have a set of holy books: the Old Testament for Judaism, the Old and New Testaments for Christianity, and the Qur'an (Koran) for Islam. The buildings of congregation and worship for these religions are called differently: synagogues for the Jews; churches for the Christians; mosques for the Muslims. Sangha is the oldest, democratically constituted, historic celibate order, founded by the Buddha. If we read the Qur'an, the debts to the Bible are unmistakable. The believers of these strands of religions looked at the other people quite differently and called pagans or heathens. The Muslims in particular could not accommodate people who did not believe in the Qur'an and despised them as infidels or unbelievers.

The Old Testament always emphasises that the foreign rule over the Jewish people is an abomination, resulting from the collective disobedience by the Jews to their God. It is strange to note that the New Testament approves the Roman rule over the Jews. The New Testament does not refer to how the Romans conquered the Jews; in fact, its narration starts after the event, and takes non-historical form unlike many of the books in the Old Testament which present the teachings in the historical contexts. The Roman governor carried out the crucifixion of Jesus Christ because Christ allegedly incited rebellion against the Roman authority. The authors of the New Testament took great pains in absolving the guilt of the execution from the Roman governor and placing all the blames on the Jewish mobs. As a matter of fact, the governor had the authority and the military clout to stop the execution. Pilate himself said to Jesus Christ, 'Don't you realise I have power either to free you or to crucify you?' (John 19:10) This shifting of the blame is one reason why the Christians persecuted the Jews for the past two millenniums, though the peoples attacked the Jews for what they were before and after the crucifixion of Christ. The pogrom was the consciousness of the Jewish people through the Old Testament and in fact the theme of the books of Esther and 3 Maccabees was the anti-Semitic pogrom, though somewhat disguised.

Though the Jews suffered under the Roman rule, the Romans recognised that Judaism had the special status in the Middle East, and their benign policy was favourable for the Jews. The fundamental reason why the Christians approved the Roman rule was that it had the favourable policy, when the New Testament was being written, for the practice and spread of their faith within the Roman Empire as the missions of Paul testifies. The authors of the books may have been also afraid of the Roman intervention if they wrote against the Roman occupation. Paul carefully left out all references to Jewish nationalism to avoid challenge to Rome. The Apostle John wrote Revelation, the last book of the New Testament, when the Christians were entering a time of persecution within the Roman Empire; he still left out all the references to the persecutions. Christ addressed his teachings to the poor and the underclass of the society. Christianity was initially the religion of the less advantaged people who became an easy target of persecution. The Christians at that time did not have any strong church organisation which they could have asked for help in the same way the Jews under the persecution by the Nazis did not have their own state they could have asked for help.

Judaism was only for the Jews who did not want to share their faith with any other peoples. However, the followers of Christianity and Islam believed in the universality of their religion and were so intent on this belief that they were prepared to go to any length as to make war for spreading their religion. This facet has shown in the crusades of the Christians and the religious wars between Catholics and Protestants in Europe in the past, and the holy wars of the Muslims in the past and present.

Philosophy based on supernatural beings is by its nature uncompromising and intolerant of the other philosophies since the former teachings come as the rigid instructions of the divinity which often does not state the reasoning behind.

The Buddhists have shown tolerance to the other denominations of Buddhism as well as to the non-Buddhist doctrines (Kennedy 1987, p. 239). The doctrinal differences of Hinayanism and Mahayanism are quite small in the overall teachings of the Buddha and often people of these creeds have shared the same monasteries. To cite an example. Though *The Dhammapada* is in Sutta Pitaka, the Pali canon, hence the Hinayana tradition: however, the Mahayana followers widely have read the canon as well. There are at present four hundred million followers of Buddhism in the world, but in the process of spreading the faith, no wars and no blood sheds to speak of were carried out. (Koller 1985, p. 239)

Arius (256-336) of Alexandria maintained that Jesus, though he was called the Son of God, did not share equally in God's divinity. Constantine the Great, fearing that Arianism may divide his empire, called for the first ecumenical council at Nicaea in 325 and declared that Jesus was one substance with the Father and Holy Spirit. Thus the Roman Empire outlawed Arianism. The Trinity became the orthodox doctrine of Christianity in the 4th century. However the further disputes took place, the regional church authorities complicating the matter.

The Council of Ephesus (AD 449) deposed Nestorius, Syrian churchman, for heresy but the issue was not settled till the Council of Chalcedon (AD 451). The council condemned the extreme form of Nestorius' teaching which upheld the semi-divinity of the Son (Jesus Christ), and was crushed within the Roman Empire and spread to the Near East, Egypt, India and China. Nestorius argued that Christ was a person but had two distinct natures, one human and one divine, and he tended to emphasise the human nature. The Nestorians as we know emphasised the human nature of Christ more than Nestorius himself put forward. In fact Muhammad claimed to be the messenger of God and denied any divinity in Jesus Christ and himself.

> The dispute as to the nature of Christ burdened Byzantine emperors since the fourth-century reign of Constantine the Great, and all efforts to resolves differences between the two sides had ultimately failed. The official position affirmed at the Council of Chalcedon in 451, held that Christ had two natures, human and divine. Monophysites insisted that he had one nature, a unity of the human and the divine. (The Editors of Time-Life Books 1988, p. 61)

Low rainfall and high temperatures characterise the Arabian Peninsula. Desert made up much of Arabia and the desert was mostly sandy but could be rocky or stony except in the southern part where some rainfall made the farming possible. In the peninsula there lived a people called the Arabs, most of whom were nomads wandering with their animals and some of whom settled on small farms near sources of water. They lived in a tribe which is no more than a large extended family group.

A boy was born into a clan in Mecca in 570. His father had died before he was born and his mother also died when he was 6. His name was Muhammad, and his uncle who became head of the clan, a subdivision of a tribe, brought him up. The boy travelled far and wide with the caravans and met the Christians and Jews who taught him about their monotheistic religions.

At the time when Muhammad started preaching his convictions to the Arabs in the early 7th century, polytheism was bound up with the tribal system through the local cults in the Arabian Peninsula. In the Arabian Desert, the beliefs tended towards spirit worship. The desert was said to be haunted by demons called jinns. The moon was seen as a benevolent spirit, and the various stars were identified with clan deities. Certain natural objects--trees, caves, desert springs, rock of unusual shape--were also venerated. (p. 28) Muhammad expressed his convictions in the Qur'an, whose major inspiration was the Bible. However, many Muslims believe in a more romantic compilation of the Qur'an as briefed in the following paragraphs.

The revelation of the Qur'an commenced in the month of Ramadan, which is the ninth month of the Arabian year. The Qur'an means a book in which is gathered all the divine books.

After marrying Khadijah, a 40 year old rich widow, when he was 25, Muhammad was still troubled by what was happening in Mecca—his personal tragedy, eroding of the family and tribal loyalty, and unacceptable manner of the Mecca's rulers. He used to retire to a cave on Mount Jabal Hira in the nearby desert every year to meditate and pray for days on end. One night in 610, during the month of Ramadan, the archangel Gabriel spoke to him, who recited and memorised everything communicated to him.

The Holy Qur'an was revealed over 23 years and some chapters were revealed complete and some fragmentary; however, the arrangement of the verses and chapters was the work of Muhammad. He continued to receive the message of God up to the time of his death. During the prophet's life the believers memorised the revelations. After his death a collection of these revelations was written down. The Qur'an also meant recitation. (Davison 1993, p. 76)

Muhammad was aware that he was both a seer and a statesman and he played the dual role well (The Editors of Time-Life Books 1988, p. 35).

Before the transformation wrought by the Qur'an, the Arabs worshipped idols, stones, trees, heaps of sand. The Arabs had been addicted to alcohol and constant tribal fighting. The Qur'an (83.14) says: Nay, rather, what they earned is rust upon their hearts. However, all these disappeared in the face of the new faith.

Muhammad preached a single god and a creed of compassion and concern in a community, based on righteousness, neither on wealth nor on power (Davison 1993, p. 75). He did not coin the word Allah. In the traditional Arab tribes, the Arabs worshiped a multitude of gods, among whom was Allah, heavenly and supreme god and the creator of the universe. Allah was the chief deity of the Quraysh tribe, the ruling tribe of Mecca, at the time of birth of Muhammad. There were 10 main clans in this tribe and Muhammad belonged to the Hashim clan.

Muhammad reportedly said to his wife, 'Angels refuse to enter a house in which there is a picture'. However, there is no precept against embroidering of typography. (The Editors of Time-Life Books 1988, p. 119)

The Arabs learned a great deal from the Byzantine Empire whose people had a great admiration to and preserved the past civilisation, particularly of the ancient to classical Greek and lesser degree of the Roman, and also acquired knowledge from the Persian Empire. Thus the Arabs made advances in the fields of medicine, algebra, geometry and astronomy, which were far ahead of the Europeans at the time. The Arabs insisted the knowledge on translating into their language, and built several libraries in the House of Wisdom in Bagdad. (Richards & English 1985, pp. 83-5) Muhammad also encouraged learning and the Muslims brought together a vast collection of knowledge, which were in turn to pass onto Western Europe.

Jihad, struggle in the way of God, implied at first spiritual battle against the temptation of Satan but it quickly took on the meaning of a holy war against non-believers.

> Under Islamic rules, the conquered peoples were allowed to keep their own laws and follow their own religious beliefs. Taxes were generally lighter than under the imperial regimes, and justice was strictly enforced. (The Editors of Time-Life Books 1988, p. 41)

Under Islamic rule, non-Muslims were subject to heavier taxes, including a head tax and levies on property.

Muhammad lived in Medina until he died in 632. He did not leave any succession rule, and on the death of the caliph it became common to result in the succession struggles. However, gradually the position of the leader became hereditary.

For the rise and spread of Islam, refer to Section 5 Crusades (1096-1291), Chapter 3, Book One *Idealism and Materialism*.

On the day of Muhammad's death, Umar, one of the most powerful Muslims, acknowledged Abu Bakr as caliph, being afraid of the division of the Islamic community, and the others followed suit. Abu Bakr (632-634) (He had the epithet of 'The Upright') became the caliph: earlier Muhammad had married Abu Bakr's daughter. Abu Bakr was of the tribe of Quraysh (Taim clan), and Muhammad's close companion and adviser. He established that the community leaders should make the religious decisions. This formed the basis of Sunni

Islam, the followers of which were called the Sunnites. The Sunnites asserted that the caliphate belong to the tribe of Quraysh, to which Muhammad belonged; however, they were pragmatic enough to accept a caliph of any origin who was able to lead the Muslim world.

Umar (634-644) succeeded Abu Bakr who had relied heavily on him during his reign and nominated him to succeed him. Umar was of Adi clan of Quraysh tribe. At the death of Umar, who was assassinated by a Persian slave for personal reasons, the council elected Uthman (644-656) as caliph. He was of Umayya clan, one of Quraysh tribe.

The policies of the Uthman caliphate were extremely unpopular among his subjects, who eventually murdered him. Ali (656-661) was chosen to become the fourth caliph. Ali was the closest living relative of Muhammad and his caliphate was the beginning of the Shiite division of Islam. Ali was of Hashim clan of Quraysh tribe and the first cousin of Muhammad. Ali's father, uncle of Muhammad, cared for Muhammad as a child. Later Muhammad adopted Ali. Ali married Muhammad's daughter, who bore two sons. There was a lifelong strong bond between the two. It was rumoured that Muhammad just before he died nominated Ali as his successor; however, the circumstances did not allow that to eventuate at that time. The Shiites ever since wanted a caliph who was Ali's lineal descendants.

The Abbasids whose dynasty ruled in Bagdad from 750 to 1258 opened schools for studying the Qur'an. The scholars compiled the body of laws called the Sharia.

Caliph was the successor to Muhammad and supposed to be both the temporal and religious leader of the entire Islamic world. The Mongol conquest of Bagdad in 1258 ended the power of the Abbasids. Mamluks were the caliphate from 1258. The Ottomans took over the title in 1517 but the Turkish republic abolished it in 1924. Today the Shiah (or the Shia), the adherents of which are called the Shiites, is the smaller of the two major divisions (the other being the Sunni) with about 10% of the Muslim followers but it is the majority faith in Iran and Iraq.

Mecca had been the centre of the Arabs' polytheistic religion when Muhammad came to settle there. In Kaaba, the temple of polytheism, was kept a black meteoric stone central to its religion and also the stone idols. It seems that the major resistance to converting to Muhammad's teaching by the people in Mecca was that they would lose the profitable business of controlling a large number of pilgrims to sacred Kaaba. Muhammad allowed Kaaba and the sacred black stone to be incorporated into Islam, after destroying all the other stones. He said that the black stone was a gift from Allah. There was also a limited spread of Judaism and Christianity in Arabia. There were a few Christians in Mecca and a large number of the Jews in Medina in the early 7th century. It seems that Muhammad acquired knowledge of the Bible from these people. (Eliade 1985, p. 63)

Muhammad's message was simple: submission to the will of a single universal god, Allah. He promised a judgment day of reward and punishment and encouraged charity to the poor.

There are popular stories which were based on the Bible and the Qur'an. Hagar, an Egyptian slave girl, and her son, Ishmael, went to Mecca, in order to escape the wrath of Sarah, their mistress. The spring there saved their life and came to be known as the well of Zamzam (Genesis 16 and 21). Abraham, Sarah's husband, visited Mecca and together with Ishmael constructed a shrine, later to be known as Kaaba, embedding in its wall a sacred black stone of meteoric origin (Qur'an 2.127) aforementioned.

Muhammad in his genius of political skills instituted various policies under his leadership. He recognised Kaaba as their sanctuary 'House of Allah'. He abolished tribal loyalty hitherto paramount in the Arab peninsula, to be replaced by a community of Muslims. Further he allowed the expansion of Islam beyond ethnic and racial frontiers. Muhammad, initially, chose Jerusalem as the point of Islamic orientation, but seeing that the Jews did not yield to his teachings, he adopted Mecca as the centre of the worship. (p. 73) The Arabs who abandoned raiding of pre-Islamic era and instead waged the holy war under Islam did so from the earthly prizes as well as for heavenly yields.

Anybody who reads both the Qur'an and the Bible realises that the founder of Islam, Muhammad, drew his major inspirations from Judaism. His favourite figure was Abraham, above mentioned, and the Muhammadans claim that Abraham is the father of the Arabs through his son Ishmael. It can be said that Muhammad integrated Islam into the Abrahamic tradition. There is some evidence to show that Nestorian Christianity also influenced Muhammad.

Islam had to come forth to satisfy the spiritual needs of the Arabs. The Arabs have been in enmity with the Jews from the biblical times to the present day. Historically their hostility centred on who would occupy the strip of land with the opening to the Mediterranean Sea, the western portion of the Fertile Crescent, apart from the enmity arising from race and possibly from trade. The Holy Qur'an says:

> O you who believe, take not the Jews and the Christians for friends. They are friends of each other. And whoever amongst you takes them for friends he is indeed one of them. Surely Allah guides not the unjust people. (Qur'an 5.51)

For the Jews this was the Promised Land flowing with milk and honey and often referred to as Canaan in the Bible. Neither side had the strength to exterminate the other through the history, unlike in the American and Australian continents where the Europeans exterminated a huge number of the native inhabitants with impunity in the modern era.

Because of the hostility, the Arabs were reluctant to take up the Bible which was nothing but the revelation of the Jewish God. The Qur'an rose to the same level in religious significance as the Old and New Testaments and at the same time ennobled the Arabic language as a liturgical and theological language. When Muhammad preached his gospel in the seventh century, the Arabs were too eager to absorb the new religion revealed in the Qur'an, after the initial resistance crumbled. The Qur'an, in addition, had the benefit of being easy to understand. The Qur'an often refers to a messenger of God in preference to an apostle of God. God is all hearing, all seeing, and all knowing in preference to omniscient; all powerful and all mighty in preference to omnipotent. The people who are familiar with the Bible may wonder if the terms used in the Qur'an may carry all the meanings originally intended. The New Testament is much easier to understand than the Old Testament, and the Qur'an is further much easier to understand than the New Testament. For this reason Islam has no priesthood who help people interpret the sacred book. Anybody can understand the fundamental messages of the Qur'an without the media of priests. The Arabs, probably by their nature, did not want complicated theology and rather had the teaching that guided them in their daily life. For example, the Arabs strictly adhered to the prohibitions of image makings. The Christians and the Buddhists alike are guilty of making images in spite of the fact that their teachings prohibited making images of anything: Christianity explicitly and Buddhism implicitly. As a matter of fact the Mahayana Buddhism permitted representation of images. The Mahayanists took the Buddha as God and worshipped him with fervent devotion, which gave rise to the expression in the art of sculpture and painting.

The Qur'an tends to avoid the complex theories and in point of fact anybody who observes the following 'pillars' of Islam can be recognised as the believer:

- daily prayer
- fasting in the month of Ramadan
- pilgrim to Mecca

- almsgiving
- a brief profession of faith: ‘There is no god but Allah and Muhammad is the messenger of Allah.’

(Kung et al. 1986, p. 46)

There are other duties such as fighting bad instincts and forbidden things, and taking part in a holy war.

The Qur’an prohibits the marriage among the close relatives (Qur’an 4.22-3). However, it permits polygamy with certain conditions.

> And you fear that you cannot do justice to orphans, marry such women as seems good to you, two or three or four; but if you fear that you will not do justice, then (marry) only one or that which your right hands possess. This is more proper that you may not do injustice. (Qur’an 4.3)
> note: That which your right hands possess means the prisoners of war.

Islam also places a strict prohibition on drinking alcohol, gambling and idolatry (e.g., Qur’an 2.219; 5.90). We all know the harms caused by excessive drinking and immoderate gambling. God is omnipresent and has no shape, and idolatry gives the impression that time and space limit God. Drawing and sculpturing God in any form also give the impression that God has a human shape. When the Bible said that God made humans in the image of God, it did not mean in the physical sense but meant in the spiritual sense.

The Bible does not give reasons why it prohibits the image makings of God. I would imagine that God is omniscient and omnipotent hence we cannot represent God in a physical form. Once people show God in the concrete forms in picture and sculpture, people are placing the limits to God. Whatever the theoretical reasons behind this prohibition, the Muslims destroyed not only the images of God but drawings, sculptures and even offensive buildings wherever they conquered, thus adhering to the teaching of the Qur’an to the letter.

There are other reasons why the Qur’an is easy to understand. The Old Testament was composed by the scores of authors who lived over a millennium apart and expressed their religious feelings in several different genres, and their views are not necessarily consistent. This is probably the major reason why the theological controversies in the Christian world arose. Jesus Christ had the Old Testament at his disposal. Also the scores of authors wrote the New Testament in the time span of half a century. As far as I am aware, the Muslims did not suffer from the major theological controversies, except in the dispute as to who would be the caliph controlling the Muslim world. One man, Muhammad, composed the Qur’an during his life time, and he also had the advantage to study the Bible as a whole and extracted only the doctrines he thought important and proper for his people and expressed in one genre of poems.

Muhammad preached holy war to convert the infidels into his faith but as the time passed, the Moslems (Muslims) were more interested in raising tributes than conversion.

The number of the Muslims in the world is estimated to be 1.3 billion in the year 2002 and 300 million of them are Arabs.

Submission to Allah in the spiritual field has a corresponding concept ‘Submit to the absolute ruler’ by Thomas Hobbes (1588-1679) in the political field. Both try to achieve the harmony in the respective field by submission.

China

Refer to Section 1 Before Establishment of Empire, Chapter 2, Book One *Idealism and Materialism* for early history of China.

> Shang kings communicated with their ancestors through sacrificial rituals and divinations.

> There were spiritual forces separate from ancestors--especially Di, the Lord on High, who could grant bountiful harvests, lend divine assistance in battle, and send rain, thunder, wind, drought or epidemics. But to communicate with these forces, the king regularly called on his ancestors to act as intermediaries. (Ebrey 1996, p. 21)

Though the first half of the Zhou (Chou) period (1111-770 BC) was nowhere near advanced as the earlier Shang era, it was a period of relative peace and security within the new feudal system. Because of this peace, the first half of the Chou was known as a golden period of China's history.

By 770 BC the society was fragmented and a coalition of feudal lords attacked the Chou capital successfully and killed the king and usurped his power. From then on the Chou kings were puppets controlled by the coalition.

The period 550 to 200 BC, historically known as the age of the 'Hundred Philosophers', was a golden age in classical Chinese thought. The four main competing intellectual schools at the time--Confucianism, Daoism (Taoism), Mohism and Legalism--offered substantially different responses to the decline and fall of the glorious Chou civilisation, an elaborate 'feudal' ritual system that had provided economic well-being, political order, social stability and cultural elegance in China proper for several centuries. (Sharma 1993, p. 148)

In the AD fourth century, Buddhism spread to China through the trade routes from Central Asia and India.

In a broader historical context, three major religions in China were traditionally Confucianism, Daoism and Buddhism. Though their presentations were certainly different, many Chinese scholars have emphasised that these three religions were essentially one tradition. Confucianism comprised of the detailed prescriptions of life but lacked the metaphysical foundation unlike Daoism and Buddhism. Confucian gentlemen were those who pursue self-cultivation in order to serve humanity. The Confucians' focal point was humans, human conducts and human organisations. The Daoists took their idea from nature and emphasised intuition and spontaneity. The focal points of humanism, naturalism and supernaturalism were humans, nature and supernatural beings. The Daoists were associated with the cult of immortality and with alchemy, looked into nature and carried out experiments and made great contributions to chemistry and metallurgy.

Confucianism developed into an orthodox set of beliefs, and stressed on filial piety, loyalty and sincerity, whereas Daoism became increasingly unorthodox and stressed on simplicity, patience and harmony.

The Daoists (Taoists) promoted Dao (Tao) meaning Way of Nature, and taught that life must be simple and peaceful, being in harmony with nature. The things, whatever they may be, should be left in their natural state, and any changes that are part of nature should take place spontaneously. Jean Jacques Rousseau (1712-1778) also emphasised the goodness of the natural state of everything. The Daoists and the Confucians differed in their fundamental outlooks of life and also in their everyday dealings.

The Confucians eventually triumphed over the Daoists with the state sponsorship, became the historians in China and came to despise Daoism and science associated with it.

> The Daoists taught that the government should leave the people alone as much as possible, not interfering in the lives of the people except when necessary for their own wellbeing (Koller 1985, p. 303).

Confucianism is in this respect in the midway between Legalism and Daoism and preached that the government should rule using the moral principles. Legalism insisted on the strict control by the government, whereas Daoism argued for the minimum control by the government.

Kongfuzi (Confucius) said, 'If you govern the people by laws and control them with punishments, they will try to keep out of trouble but will have no sense of shame. If you govern them with virtue and control them with ceremony, they will have a sense of shame and correct themselves'. He further said, 'I am no better than others in dealing with law suits. The thing is to do away with them'. (Chien 1979, p. 437)

Laozi (Lao-tzu), the founder of Daoism, said, 'The man of superior virtue does not lay stress on virtue and so he has virtue. The man of inferior virtue clings to virtue and so he has no virtue. The more laws are promulgated, the more brigands and thieves there will be. When men of low understanding hear about the Way, they laugh out loud at it'. He also said, "Unless one knows and lives according to the inner laws of the universe, which he calls the 'invariables', one ends up in a disaster". (p. 437) This invariables is akin to the biblical God, and truth in general usage. In China, the tradition of Confucianism and even of Daoism established that the human world is primary and the world of things is of secondary importance.

The Grand Historian [Sima Qian (Ssu-ma Ch'ien)] comments: Laws and codes are instruments of government, but not the cause of good government (p. 437).

Confucius descended from the Shang aristocrats who were herded into Sung at the defeat of Western Chou in the late 12th century BC. His grandfather fled from Sung to the state of Lu, where Confucius was born. The Duke of Chou was the original ruler of Lu. Confucius was interested in the preservation of the culture of the ancestors. Confucius and Mencius looked to the past for the models how the rulers should behave. Confucius took the Duke of Chou (only 500 years before his time) as his ideal ruler. (Milston 1978, pp. 92, 94)

Confucius stressed the familial virtues, especially the filial love. It is on history that as the result of the deference to mother, a Chinese emperor often consulted Empress Dowager, emperor's mother or grandmother, on policy matters and was frequently overruled. In the family, the infants form their character and the fundamental attitudes towards the other people and society. Without proper education within the family, Confucius reasoned, it was not possible to form the peaceful and stable society. Demophilus, an ancient Greek, also stressed the importance of education and wrote, 'Education is like a golden crown; it confers both honour and profit' (Harbottle 1897, p. 387).

Confucius reached a high level of wisdom. His teaching centres on the concept of ren (jen) which is often rendered as humility, benevolence or perfect wisdom. Ren is based on basic human nature. He defined ren as love of mankind, and goodness as the practice of ren. Confucius in a dialogue equated humanity with loving of people, and knowledge with knowing people. 'As a general virtue jen means humanity, i.e., that which makes a man moral being. As a particular virtue, it means love.' (Chan 1963, p. 40) The term as Confucius used has more active meaning and I would translate it as 'Love thy neighbour', referring not only to the correct attitudes to the other people but virtues in the general sense. Ren includes such teaching as 'Honour your parents', since Confucius taught that the filial piety or the children's reverence towards their parents is the root of all virtues. Cicero similarly wrote: Filial piety is the foundation stone of all virtues (Harbottle 1897, p. 212). If the parents show the proper humanity to their children by their example, the children naturally follow the lead. If the family is governed properly, it is expected that the whole country is governed properly. Beginning with himself and his family, he first made himself master in his own house; a thing which is, in many cases, as difficult as the ruling of a province [Tacitus] (p. 1). The worst ruler is the man who is unable to rule himself [Cato Major] (p. 399). For whoso his own household ruleth ill, how shall he hope to render aid without [Euphron]? (p. 428) Confucius thought that goodness, wisdom and courage are virtues, and they characterise the gentlemen or superior men. The superior person has a developed humanity and is inwardly cultivated. The inferior person acts on instinct and for profit. People should not act according to likes and dislikes but should live according to ren (jen). He said, 'He who is really good is never unhappy'. He also said, 'The superior man understands the higher things [moral principles]; the inferior man the lower things [profit]'. (Chan 1963, p. 42) He moreover thought the superior men's proper career is to govern.

Confucius said referring to himself:

> A transmitter and not a maker, believing in and loving ancient studies (Chen 1987, p. 23).

Confucius said:

> Learning without thinking is labour lost; thought without learning is perilous (p. 36).
> Virtue is adoption of the Way and consists of wisdom, benevolence and courage. Wisdom aims at the knowledge of benevolence and courage in its practice. (p. 88)

Confucius said:

> He who possesses sincerity hits what is right without an effort and apprehends without thinking; he is the sage who embodies the Way with calm and ease (p. 192).

The Doctrine of the Mean reads: Sincerity is the Way of Heaven. The Christian Bible says: God is in Heaven and God is the Way. (p. 195)

Confucius said:

> Is the mean not perfect as a virtue? For a long time few have had it.
> To go beyond is as wrong as to fall short. (p. 219)

In Confucianism, neither empty words nor fine words constitute benevolence. It is only by vigorous conduct that benevolence can be manifested. (p. 239) Benevolence is love of men.

The philosopher Yu said:

> Filial piety and fraternal submission are the root of benevolence (p. 257).

Confucius said:

> The superior man is modest in his speech, but exceeds in his actions. Also, the superior man wishes to be slow in his speech and quick in his conduct. (p. 258)

Confucius said:

> The superior man has neither anxiety nor fear (p. 259).

Prayer is a form of self-examination. Confucius himself prayed, and he advised his disciples to do so constantly, not only on specific occasions.

Psychologists report that the first years of human life are the most important for establishing basic attitudes and behavioural patterns of humans. In this respect too the family is the most important factor in forming the characters of humans who comprise the society. The family is the basic stable unity of society, and traditionally the most influential.

Confucius (551-479 BC) and Lao-tzu (?604-?531 BC) lived in the contemporary society and it is said that they met in Chou.

In China, religious traditions are not distinct from moral practices, philosophical doctrines, social customs and folklores. Two enduring structures in China, the family and the bureaucracy, have shaped the Chinese society. Confucianism should in turn guide these two pillars, the ardent Confucians through the centuries argued.

The Great Learning was written by Tseng Shen, a disciple of Confucius, and is a unique record of Confucian teachings. Zi Si (Tzu Ssu), a grandson of Confucius, wrote *The Doctrine of the Mean.*

Confucius was born in the duchy of Lu, in what is now Shandong Province. He was orphaned at an early age and grew up poor, but became the most learned man through self-education. He was made governor of one of the towns in Lu, though he was over fifty at the time. Since his administration was so successful he was promoted to Minister of Justice for the whole state at the age of fifty six. However, his political career short lived. Though he was loyal to Duke Ting of Lu, his political views did not sit well with the power holders of the duke, who entertained him with pleasures, and he was alienated. He left the country and searched for his master for 12 years without success. He returned to Lu and devoted his time for teaching and writing.

Confucius edited *The Book of Poetry* and *The Book of History*, compiled *The Book of Rites,* annotated *The Book of Changes* and wrote *The Spring and Autumn Annals*. These were called 'Five Classics'.

'Confucianism emphasised that everyone has and should accept social duty and responsibility.' (Sharma 1993, p. 280) Confucianism is without doubt pro-establishment and authoritarian, as evidenced by such precepts as 'Love thy neighbour' and 'Honour your parents'. Confucius looked to the past for his inspirations to cure the woes of the contemporary society and he thought that the society of the Western Chou (1111-770 BC) as ideal. Confucius is said to 'transmit but does not create'. That means the end of innovation and revolution. The transmission included not only specific rituals and values but also a hierarchical social structure and insight of the past. Confucius said, 'I am not someone who was born wise. I am someone who loves the ancients and tries to learn from them' (Ebrey 1996, p. 46). Because of these tendencies the various governing bodies in Asia used the Confucian doctrines to be taught at school.

Early in the Han dynasty, primarily through the efforts of the prime minister Dong Zhongshu (Tung Chung-shu) (179-104 BC) Confucianism became the state philosophy. He also instituted the civil service examination system based on Confucian doctrines to recruit the able men for the state administration. In addition, he helped found the Imperial University, where Confucian texts were the bases of all education. (Koller 1985, p. 304) 'In 136 BC, the Martial Emperor [Emperor Wudi] (140-86 BC) set up five Erudites of the Five Classics at court and in 124 BC, assigned 50 official students to study with them, thus creating a de facto imperial university. By 50 BC, the student enrolment at the university had grown to an impressive three thousand, and by AD 1, a hundred men a year were entering government service through the examinations administered by the state.' (p. 162)

Confucianism is a set of classics aforementioned. Though most of the above classics existed before Confucius, he is attributed to writing or editing some of them. His own statements collected in *Analects* (*Lun yu*) were not yet admitted into the canon. Fundamentally it was the teaching of pro-establishment and authoritarianism that the Han rulers welcomed the doctrines as the state ideology, and the decision reflected the vested interest of the ruling minority. Confucianism mainly addresses to the governing class and teaches in essence how to govern effectively and ethically. In this respect Confucianism shares the teaching of the Christian Bible. While the Bible, especially the New Testament, is the product of the proletarians, originally anyway, the book as a whole does not object to the existing authority but rather recommend subjugation to the ruling authority. The following verses expressly underline the point: You shall not revile God or curse a leader of your people (Exodus 22:28) and let every person be subjected to the government authorities; for there is no authority except from God, and those authorities that exist have been instituted by God (Romans 13:1). Also the New Testament takes the format that the Jews approve the Roman Rule over them. This attitude of pro-establishment is one reason why the Communists fiercely attacked Confucianism and Christianity.

Confucianism reflected the vested interest of the succeeding ruling minority as the official ideology of China. The rulers adopted it as the path of emolument for the bright young men through the examination system. The youths were placed in the two conflicting dilemmas. One was the quest for truth as Confucius discoursed in the form of self-cultivation and social responsibility. The other was the lure of the social advancement sacrificing the former. (Sharma 1993, p. 162) Imposition of Confucian classics in the examination system involves the deception by the government, and the examinees in turn exhibited deception being anxious to get the pass mark to get lucrative official positions.

> Buddhism arrived in China along with commercial goods, following trade routes from northern India through the Buddhist kingdoms of Central Asia such as Khotan and Kucha (Ebrey 1996, p. 96).
>
> The Sui emperor Wen had seen Buddhism as a portent weapon in his ideological armoury and elevated the faith to a status approaching state religion. But Taizong [T'ai-tsung] saw in Buddhism an alarming potential for subversion. In Buddhism's nirvana, there was no room for the Sons of Heaven as Chinese emperors styled themselves. (The Editors of Time-Life Books 1988, p. 109)

It is ironical to see what sort of a person Taizong was. He at the age of 25 killed two of his brothers--one, the Crown Prince--and forced his aging father Gaozu (Kao Tsu), the first Tang (T'ang) emperor, to abdicate, becoming an emperor himself in 626. However, he proved to be a just and wise ruler, as well as a deft politician and a military genius. He ushered in an era of unprecedented peace and prosperity in T'ang China.

> His conduct approached so closely the Confucian ideal that later Chinese historians made the name of his reign, True Vision, a byword for good government. To recruit the most capable persons, he set up the civil service examination system. The Board of Civil Office in Changan [Ch'ang-an] held the examinations annually--and opened them to virtually all literate candidates. The subject included history, the Confucian classics, poetry, administration and government. (p. 104)

Legalism first appeared in the state of Ch'i (the present-day Shandong Province) in the 7th century BC. The state of Ch'i was a Chou domain and the Ch'in state conquered Ch'i in 221 BC. Ch'in had nominated Legalism as their state policy in the 4th century BC. Henceforth Legalism was always associated with Ch'in, particularly Shi huang-ti. The policy of this emperor came from Li Ssu, First Minister, and one of his most notorious decrees was an order to burn all non-Legalist books.

Hanfeizi (Han-fei-tzu) (d. 233 BC) formulated the Legalist philosophy which was already several hundred years old. The fundamental premise of the school was that people were basically evil hence the law and punishment had to regulate them. The law for this school was a vehicle for morality. He began as a student of Confucianism and analysed Legalism from the perspective of the ruler.

The main writings on Legalism, for example, *The Book of Lord Shang* (4th century BC), centre in statecraft: how a ruler should conduct in order to make the state powerful and secure. They are often compared to *The Prince* by Machiavelli.

The Legalists bitterly attacked the Confucians and Mohists but did not attack the Daoists. One reason lay in the fact that some aspects of the Legalist doctrines originated in the Daoist philosophy, though the control by and superiority of the state were entirely incompatible with Daoism. (Chan 1963, pp. 254-5)

Mohism is the religious and ethical teaching of Mozi (Mo-tzu) and emphasises universal love, ascetic self-discipline, and obedience to the will of Heaven. The teaching has an aspect of the utilitarian spirit of the modern interest and has a superficial resemblance to Christianity. (p. 212) The Mohists established communities similar to Christian church. They lived separate from the general community; running their own affairs, holding religious services and following their laws. The Mohist school as such disappeared from the society after the 3rd century BC, though its teachings were absorbed into Confucianism and Daoism.

There are two texts associated with Daoism. *The Classic on the Way and Its Power* was attributed to Lao-tzu who presumably lived during the sixth century BC. Zhuangzi (Chuang-tzu) (c. 370-301 BC) wrote *Zhuangzi* (*Chuang-tzu*). These books represent philosophical phase of Daoism in contrast with the later development of religious phase. (Lopez 1996, p. 8)

The imperial Chinese family sometimes supported Daoism. 'For example, at various points of the reign of Li family during T'ang dynasty [618-907], prospective candidates for government service were tested for their knowledge of specific Taoist scriptures.' (p. 11) Li Yuan (later Emperor Gaozu), founder of the T'ang dynasty, claimed descent from Lao-tzu.

Though the Daoists emphasised the quest for immortality, it also stressed morality. The Daoists stressed specific injunctions against stealing, lying and taking life as well as abstract discussions of virtue. (p. 12)

The Daoists despised the Confucians and ever made fun of them. The concept of God as familiar to the Christians appears in the Daoist book *The Book of Recompenses* which was addressed to the governed and was also universally read:

> The connections between actions and their consequences is the mysterious law of God--the changeless decree pronounced by the Judge of the unseen world (Sheowring and Thies 1982, p. 71).

Laozi (Lao-tzu) reasoned:

> As human beings grow and learn, they become habituated and complicated, losing their openness and flexibility. Hence he recommended that we return to infancy and become 'uncarved blocks'. (McGreal 1995, p. 15)

The Bible makes the similar recommendation.

Daoism teaches that noblepersons are not enticed by likes and oppressed by dislikes. The epithets of Dao (Tao) are:

Chaos
Emptiness
Nothingness
The Great
The One

The above epithets have elements to remind us Buddhism and Christianity.

Dao is empty like a bowl, without characteristics and particularities and at the same time with the possibility of characteristics and particularities.

Daoism lectures, 'Only that which exists from the very beginning of the universe and neither dies nor declines until heaven and earth disintegrate can be called eternal' (Chan 1963, p. 261). This passage reminds us of Christ saying, 'Heaven and earth will pass away, but my words will not pass away' (Matthew 24:35).

The Daoists had the conviction that the government was a necessary evil and unlike Confucianism, they did not think it proper to meddle into politics as a principle. Daoist experiments in alchemy were the beginning of science in China, and Chinese science was far advanced of the West till the Renaissance. (Cotterell & Morgan 1975, p. 36)

> Taoist philosophy is basically anti-traditional and a guide for the weak caught up in the social competition. It is, therefore, more attractive to those who do not have fortune on their side than to those who strive to retain their fortune and success. In over two thousand years, only one branch of Taoist philosophy has become the main current of political life—the Huang-Lao School, in the early half of the second century BC (former Han dynasty). *The Huai Nan Tzu* is the most important book of the Huang-Lao School in Han China. (Sharma 1993, pp. 234, 252)

The policies under Daoist school are lessening both taxes and forced labour, and these policies were possible because early part of the former Han dynasty was a time of peace.

Traditionally the Chinese preferred to use the term 'heaven' rather than 'god' when they referred to superior force on human destiny. The Confucians thought that Heaven does not interfere into the human affairs, and sought after moral life and the concept of Heaven, the end products of the philosophers, for their own sake.

The Son of Heaven in the Chinese context is akin to the Son of God in the Christian tradition: Both are figures of speech in the similar way that 'All roads lead to Rome' is, and indicate the person's conformity to the Way of Heaven or God. The Son of God in the New Testament refers to Jesus Christ who embodied God like natures, and the Son of Heaven refers to the successive Chinese emperors, though only one reigning emperor of Chinese stock at one time was the idealised norm.

Any unknown power which controls the affairs of people is Heaven. According to Mencius, what is done without people's doing is from Heaven. He said, 'No, Heaven does not speak. It simply showed its will by his personal conduct and his conduct of affairs'. (Chen 1987, p. 60) Confucius was insistent that the superior man conforms to the ordinances of Heaven. The superior men are the virtuous or the men of principle, practising the teaching of 'Love thy neighbour' and, in today's parlance, are the persons who treat their fellow humans as human beings. The Way of Heaven is the spiritual guidance for the common good, and in part appears as instinct for survival and prosperity or in accordance with nature and in part fostered by education and cultivation. Its focal point is benevolence or love. (p. 87)

Di [Ti] means God and Shang Di means High God or God on High. Living people cannot approach directly Di or any of the heavenly deities but only the ancestors can intercede for them. This is the main reason why the Chinese people have offered sacrifices to their ancestors through their history.

Neo-Confucianism came about in the Middle Ages of the Chinese history in response to the development of Buddhism in China. Zhou Dunyi (Chou Tun-i) (1017-1073) laid the foundation of Neo-Confucianism but the two brothers, Cheng Hao (Ch'eng Hao) (1032-1085) and Cheng Yi (Ch'eng I) (1033-1107) gave it the enduring structure. (Cotterell & Morgan

1975, pp. 306, 310) Neo-Confucianism represents a harmonising of Confucianism and Daoism, caused by a catalyst of Buddhism.

Chu Hsi (1130-1200), a great Neo-Confucian, compiled *Four Books*; consisting of *The Great Learning*, *The Doctrine of the Mean*, *The Confucian Analects* and *The Works of Mencius*. He made many enemies by his frank opinions and his uncompromising attacks on corruption and political expediency. As a consequence his political career had serious difficulties and eventually came to a halt. After his death *Four Books* were adopted as the basic sources of examination questions and came to be read more widely than *Five Classics*.

> The traditional Confucian contempt for popular religion, whether Taoism or Buddhism, was taken a stage further by Chu Hsi, who denied that there was a personal deity. 'There is', he said, 'no man in heaven judging sin'. Instead a moral force, an impersonal power, ruled the universe; the duty of mankind was cooperation with its workings, since they were the laws of Nature. (p. 127)

Zhu Xi's (Chu Hsi's) ideas (the foregoing and others) profoundly affected the European scholars of the Enlightenment (p. 128).

Wang Yangming (Wang Yang-ming) (1472-1529) was the most brilliant representation of Neo-Confucian ideals. (p. 321)

Religions were born from the self-preservation of the protagonists and looked into their mind for the various solutions and hence generally pro-establishment. Because of this stance, the spread of religions was comparatively easy. The communists, though guided similarly by the instinct of self-preservation, looked at the existing establishment as the order to be replaced with the new order and consequently experienced serious frictions wherever they preached communism.

Since every race appears to have a concept of deity, it must be something fundamental to human existence in the same way as languages are. The spoken words are obviously futile if they are unheard, misheard or misunderstood. Further the words, spoken or written, are futile and illusory unless they are in accord with facts or truths.

In later Palaeolithic and Neolithic times, articulate speech developed among humans, which gave them mental hand-hold for consecutive thought and an enlargement of co-operation (Wells 1925, p. 115).

Languages have come into existence for an obvious reason: to communicate effectively. F Engels wrote that the human language originated in the process of labour, thus enhancing the importance of labour which he argued was the source of all value. He also argued that the characteristic difference of men from monkeys is nothing but labour. He further wrote that the results of labour by the ancient people can be seen in the tools they left, that is, hunting and fishing implements, sometimes used as weapons. (Marx & Engels 1970, pp. 68, 70-1)

All humans often use quite effectively non-verbal means to communicate under certain circumstances. Photographs and comic pictures often convey what the languages cannot. Languages are not characteristics of humans since the mammals and birds have spoken languages of their own though simple, to satisfy their communicative needs. The mammalians and feathered creatures use simple verbal and non-verbal methods to effect the transmissions of their emotions--warning of danger, expression of love, display of anger and so forth. They may also utter voices purely for pleasure as we sing songs. They don't need complicated system of exchange because they don't have any complicated ideas to start with. In this respect they are similar to the human babies who use simple communicative device to effect uncomplicated emotional outlets.

According to the linguist Noam Chomsky, our predisposition for language is innate, that is, built into our brain. Because no one as yet worked out how language is learned, let's say children learn language by using it. No one, least of all average mother, knows how to teach it to them. (Rico 1983, pp. 51-2)

Ernest Thompson Seton, a keen animal lover, reveals his observations in his book *Wild Animals I Have Known* (1898) that the mammals and birds show some kind of moral values at times apart from the instincts and crude language capabilities. He also narrates that some birds collect shells for aesthetic reason; foxes tease humans at times; some animals risk their lives to mock their predators; and they all show unfailing parental affections to their offspring as humans do. However, the concept of divinity is totally absent from their life: their occasional moral displays come naturally to them and can be more a sign of nature rather than the belief in higher order. Why do human beings think about deity? Only humans are capable of postulating divinity. Deity or divinity must be something connected to a higher intelligence that is peculiar to men and women.

Section 3 Universality of Divinity

In the process of developing the religious cultures, the ancient peoples relied on the various means in the absence of the established wisdom. For example, people sacrificed animals or even humans as rituals in many parts of the world to pacify deities and possibly to ward off death by bartering the lives of animals or humans, and in the process people had to call on the mediums, shamans or prophets. These practices are non-consequential in that we modern people do not have to resort to the above performances to be religious. The term 'consequential' is used to denote the means of or the paths to religion which we modern people can accommodate without a doubt.

The ancients universally undertook sacrifices of animals and humans, though people no longer look at sacrifices as a duty of humans towards divinity today. Sacrifices were important duties of the rulers in the ancient world and only the select few carried out the sacrificial duties and these people in turn professed to have received the instructions from the divinity to pass to the other people. The Bible makes frequent references to the kinds of animal sacrifices the ruler-priests have to conduct, though it places a strict prohibition on the human sacrifices.

The 'oracle texts' or 'oracle bone inscriptions' were the earliest written records of religious observance in China. They date from the Shang dynasty (18-12 century BC). The oracle texts record the sacrifices of a large number of animals and even humans. These records show that the last Shang rulers ceased to view divination as an effective means of spirit communication in contrast with the earlier generations. Because the royal ancestors were in many cases the former rulers of the state, the communication with these spirits were in fact the form of ancestor worship, the most widely spread form of religious practice in traditional China. (Lopez 1996, pp. 41-4)

> In China, the death of parents marks the end of the son's service to them while alive and the beginning of his service to them after their lives ended. Sacrifices are aimed at the remembrance of those who are loved and reverenced. They take place on anniversaries of the birth and death of the deceased. (Chen 1987, pp. 397, 404)

The ancient to classical peoples also showed their reverence to god by building huge pyramids as in Egypt, large and elaborate temples as in Egypt and the Levant, and Roman and Greek cities.

Fasting was a religious observance as universal as prayer among the Jews, Hindus, Christians and Muslims. Fasting is still a prominent practice in the Muslim faith today.

The Qur'an (Koran) has the following passage, extolling the value of charity:

> If you manifest charity, how excellent it is! And you hide it and give it to the poor, it is good for you. And it will do away with some of your evil deeds; and Allah is aware of what you do. (Qur'an 2.271)

To kill the hunted beast or, later, the domesticated animal, is equivalent to a sacrifice. People ate what they sacrificed; hence, sacrifice of the animal meant in effect life for the humans. In this sense, but by no means covers all forms of sacrifice, sacrifice meant ceremonial eating.

In the world of 10 000 years ago, that is, in the primitive Neolithic age when the agriculture was beginning to develop, people carried out the human sacrifices in relation to sowing. Scholars gave a few other plausible reasons behind the human sacrifice. The human sacrifice prevailed throughout the Neolithic period in the south and middle American continent. These American tribes remained at the level of Neolithic Age when the Europeans discovered them and they too had the custom of human sacrifices in conjunction with sowing maize (or corn) which is quite different plant from the old world. The Aztec (Mexican) civilisation performed the human sacrifices in a vast scale. (Wells 1925, pp. 64, 81, 105)

> Aztecs believed that disasters could only be averted by offering Huitzilopochtli, the chief of their gods, the most valuable of all gifts--human life (Roberts 1973, p. 63).

Today the religious people may think that they can avert disasters only by cleansing their spirit and lead a good life. However, this concept may not be superior to such deeds as offering sacrifices, building monuments, praying, fasting and giving charity; they are all the means to express the reverence to divinity. We may not be able to conclude that one method is better or worse than the others, and the people may be judged by the depth of the reverence rather than the means in the same way the respect to a person may be gauged by their depth rather than the means of expressing it.

Adolf Hitler as Fuehrer was more delighted when his subordinates showed their blind devotions rather than their orderly subordination to him. God (Truth) would feel the same way, if figuratively expressed. Also the person in love wants to see the sweetheart show the blind love in whatever ways it may be. The following biblical teaching reinforces the foregoing observations: ... the Lord delights in those who fear him, who put their hope in his unfailing love (Psalms 147:11).

Today people offer flowers on wedding, funeral and other special occasions, and not animals or humans. People don't think much about its purpose but they think lots about what sort of flowers they should offer and in what way. Offering flowers today is an accepted way of life in the same way the ancients offered animals and humans as sacrifices. The ancients did not think much about its purpose and they paid attention only what to offer and in what way.

The essence of Christianity and Buddhism are not in ethics as the chapters to follow explain the ideas in detail. Section 1, Chapter 2 expounds that the core theory of Judaism-Christianity-Islam is the notion that we are judged by how close to God (Truth) irrespective of our conducts. Section 2, Chapter 3 expounds that the core theory of Buddhism is the concept that things are as appear to our mind and hence everything is an illusion. We can explain the aforementioned concept using these ideas. After all the ethics may not be important as many religious people advocate. God judges us depending on how distant or close to God, whether we dedicate in animal or human sacrifices, in building monuments, in praying, in fasting, in charity, in training our minds or in practising the morals.

Ethics itself is useless, and only the right thinking of the ethical individuals are conducive to the destinies of the human beings. We can say the same thing about the above various dedications. We get the rewards or punishments according to the setting of our minds rather than the conducts which can be seen by other people but only the genuine intentions can be perceived by God.

Idealism represented by the precept 'Love thy neighbour' is only one way of reaching to the absolute or the ultimate, that is, God (Truth). Individually idealism has nothing to do with success or failure within the society such as shown in being rich or poor, powerful or without power, and high or low ranking within the firm. In Book One I make a proposition as to the cause of decline of China proper and rise of Western Europe in the modern era that it was the diffusion depths of idealism in the two currents of civilisations. In the religious point of view that may not be the case. It may be more to do with closeness to or separateness from God (Truth). The success or failure of an individual in the society is too complicated to be judged by idealism or religion. As far as my personal experience goes what happened to me was so extraordinary to defy any logical explanation that I have no choice but to ascribe them to the works of God (Truth).

However, there is no question that idealism held by a large number of people promotes the advancement of the society as a whole over the centuries.

The universality of deity means that the religions the world over were concerned with the absolute, the ultimate, God and Heaven. Though peoples expressed their religions differently they are all manifestations of survival instinct. Underscoring the innate human need for religious beliefs there are common threads running through the religious thinking the world over. Book One *Idealism and Materialism* stresses this point in Section 3, Chapter 7, and I summarise the essence of idealism in the following messages. Note that the religion as I understand is the crystallisation of and separate from idealism.

A Love Your Neighbour as Yourself and Resulting Moral Codes
B Reward and Punishment for Thought and Conduct
C Middle Paths
D Conformance of Speech and Conduct
E Indifference to External (Physical and Mental) Stimuli

Philosophy may be the search for wisdom. Religion is a message or the way to salvation and concerns itself with the utterly final and true reality such as the Absolute, God or nirvana (Kung et al. 1986, p. xvi).

Confucius said, 'At fifteen my mind was set on learning. At thirty my character had been formed. At forty I had no more perplexities. At fifty I knew the Mandate of Heaven. At sixty I was at ease with whatever I heard. At seventy I could follow my heart's desire without transgressing moral principles' (Chan 1963, p. 22). The above passage is from *Analects* (*Lun yu*) which is a collection of Confucius dialogues. He also said, according to *Analects*, 'Heaven is the author of the virtue that is in me' and 'Virtues in secrets do not fail to show up as good news'. The Mandate of Heaven referred to is possibly akin to Will of God as we know in Judaism, Christianity and Islam. It is also akin to the concept expressed by Manilius in the following sentence: Man must be so weighed as though there were a God within him (Harbottle 1897, p. 96). Confucius must have realised at the age of fifty that the moral codes he had upheld was not a haphazard teaching but actually came from higher order, that is, Heaven. Confucius often prayed and regularly carried out rituals, and preached the importance of these matters. Confucianism looks like an ethical system of human creation but the concept of Heaven tries to justify it, and Confucius was religious under these observations. His discovery matches with the Old Testament: it presents the Ten Commandments as not human creation but the revelations from Jehovah (Yahweh).

Confucius said, 'Nobody understand me. Only Heaven understands me' (Chien 1979, 24). He was convinced, shortly before his death, that his mission had been a total failure. He had, reportedly, 3000 disciples but a maximum of 70 was more likely. The best source to know the life of Confucius may be *Analects*. *Annals of Tso* (3rd century BC), *Mencius* (probably written by the disciples of Mencius during the late 4th century BC); and *Historical Records* (1st century BC) by Ssu-ma Ch'ien also gives some accounts.

Confucius placed a sharp contrast between morally right and wrong and what we should do or not do and they become personal attributes of: spiritual men and base men; interior men and exterior men; eternal men and temporal men; spiritual men and worldly men; big men and small men; worthy men and worldlings.

In the ancient China, probably as in any other parts of the world, people conceived the earth as a source of agrarian fertility. People often referred to it as Mother Earth, indicating that it gives life to people. Similarly people referred to the sky, being the source of weather which controlled the crop fertility, as Heaven. Earth and Heaven were integral parts of cosmic totality. We can see this union in the Genesis of the Bible (Genesis 1:1-31). Also Zeus in the Greek mythology was a sky god, implying his importance identifying him with the sky which was the source of vital weather affecting life and death.

Of all the gods of the Altaic peoples, the most important is Tangri, which means god or sky. Tangri has had an immense influence over the northern part of Asia from the prehistory. Tangri created men, who lived happily until the evil spirits spread sickness and death upon the earth. Tangri did not have temples nor statute. This god is omniscient and the entire universe is the house of Tangri. One would sacrifice horses, cattle and sheep to him. In fact 'sacrifice to celestial gods is universally attested especially in cases of calamity or natural catastrophe'. People thought the shamans, in their ecstasy, to ascend to Heaven and descend to Hell. The shamanic miracles stimulated people's imagination, abolished the barriers between dreams and reality, and opened the mind towards the world inhabited by the gods, the dead and the spirits. (Eliade 1985, pp. 3-5, 21)

> The act of transport or transformation allows shamans to act as cures, spirit mediums, diviners, prophets or magicians. Forms of shamanism are still practiced in Japan, Korea and Siberia, and shamanistic belief continues to be an important component of many native American cultural traditions. (Murowchick 1994, p. 55)
>
> Because shamanism is so interwoven with other aspects of Manchu culture, scholars argue that shamanism forms the foundation of the cultural traditions of the Manchu as well as other Tungus groups in north-eastern China (Lopez 1996, p. 224).

The sun was also venerated as the source of life. The sun worship in Egypt and Inca Empire is well documented. The epithet of Louis XIV is the Sun King indicating the immense power he yielded as a sovereign.

In Judaeo-Christian-Islamic system of religions, the concept of God plays a dominant role; in Buddhism and Confucianism the concept of God or Heaven takes the back seat. *Book of Documents* (or *Classic of History*), one of the Five Confucian Classics, says, 'Those who rely on virtue will prosper, those who rely on force will perish' (Chien 1979, p. 68). This is in accord with the teaching of the Bible where God makes sure that is the case. Confucianism often implies but not necessarily expresses the will of Heaven.

Hinduism has neither churches nor binding dogmas, and only the traditions guide the followers. It embraces sacrificial cults, polytheism and monotheism.

There are different approaches to deity. The Christians face God as the repentant sinners, the Muslims as obedient slaves, while the Hindus encounter their god primarily as a Host. Euripides wrote, 'There is a god within us' (Harbottle 1897, p. 393). 'Moreover, there is, within the psyche of any single human being, a psychic universe that is apparently proving at least as vast, in its own medium, as the physical universe is.' (Toynbee et al. 1968, p. 82)

Within the confines of Buddhism and Christianity a large number of denominations are in existence, each claiming to be the true faith, hence naturally the systems of varied religions the world over hold different theories as to the nature and doctrines of their faith.

Christianity--especially the Catholic Church--has aimed at the unitary system of doctrines through its life. The Christians and the church did not tolerate any dissenting views and always tried to resolve the differences to form a uniform theory. In contrast, Buddhism developed in an entirely different way. There have been difference of Hinayanism and Mahayanism; however, many eminent Buddhist theoreticians developed their own views which may or may not express the above distinctions. I would say that there was no will to create the unified views in Buddhism unlike Christianity. The Christians had one book of the

Bible to consult and if somebody expressed a view not conforming to the established doctrines, the Christians would vigorously dispute the view. There are thousands of the Buddhist canons. The Buddhists may incorporate the new and differing view, provided of course it matches with their way of life. For the Judaics, Christianity was the dissenting doctrines: for the Christians, Islam was the dissenting view. These three different interpretations and presentations were incompatible if we follow the believers of each religion though the fundamentals of their religions are the same.

Another reason why the Christians did not tolerate the dissenting view may have been that the Christian faith was tied with the government. The king or emperor was afraid that the dissenting voice might disrupt the unification of the kingdom or empire. Constantine the Great painfully showed this concern and called for the ecumenical councils to resolve the differences.

The Russians did not understand Christianity as the Western Europeans did and were deeply involved in rituals and superstitions.

I have been convinced that the ancient Egyptians were as religious as the ancient Jews but the former expressed the religious feelings by constructing the massive buildings such as pyramids and temples. Also according to Plutarch, the Egyptians worshipped animals for their good qualities: for example, they saw patience and usefulness in ox and liveliness in cat (Montaigne 1965, p. 317). The ancient peoples the world over also expressed their religious sentiments by sacrificing animals and even humans. The following citations are from the medieval to modern age of the European world views and are well documented.

The Toltecs, c. 900-1200, and Aztecs, c. 1300-1520, were dominant in Mesoamerica. The Toltecs were noted for military prowess and expansion and human sacrifices. The Aztecs shocked the Spanish conquisitors by the wholesale human sacrifices. There were temples dedicated to the sun god Huitzilopochtli which they had to feed with human sacrifices. (Mercer 1996, p. 343) In the Inca Empire situated in Peru, c. 1100-1530s, religious ceremonies were numerous. They usually involved animal sacrifices, and carried out human sacrifices only in small scale on rare occasions. (Whitehouse & Wilkins 1986, p. 32)

It is hard for us to fathom why people expressed the religious feelings as the zeal for building the large and/or elaborate monuments or sacrificing animals and humans. *Iliad* narrates that the sacrificers as well as the gods feasted on the burning animals (Eliade 1978, p. 258). The Old Testament tells us similarly. It expresses the Jewish faith as the temple building through King Solomon as well as the rebuilding of the temple after returning in three groups from the captivity in Babylonia and joining the Jews who were not deported to Babylonia. The first temple, Solomon's Temple, in Jerusalem was destroyed by the Babylonians, and Herod built the second temple on the same site. Wailing Wall is the remaining wall of the second temple destroyed by the Romans.

However, the number of human sacrifices conducted in the Aztec civilisation far outweighed the above consideration and defies our logical explanation. That was their way of life whether it brought happiness or goodness to the conducting community. The Aztecs carried out the rituals indicating that the Sun needed human nourishment. However, the true intent may have been, as some scholars conjectured, that the overpopulation forced the killings, or the people so enjoyed eating thc human flcsh after the rituals that they simply could not stop. Laying of the flowers at the tomb today may be parallel to sacrifice in that people did not care about the deep significance, if any, but they did it by sheer custom.

The religious feelings of the ancients of many parts of the world were quite different from those of today. Probably we are wrong to pass our judgment of right or wrong on the religious peoples of entirely different life views coming from different environments. Many people today may equate the religion to the ethics, but I have found that the sentiment is misguided. The moral life may not be as good as the religious people tend to think and may not be superior to building large and/or elaborate monuments and sacrificing animals or humans in order to reach the absolute truth or God. In fact some historically eminent Christians such as St Augustine and Luther insisted that moral life have nothing to do with the salvation of the souls.

Romans 9:32 says; Israel pursued it [a righteousness] not by faith but as if it were by works. It goes on; this was the reason why Israel stumbled. Martin Luther asserted further. People cannot earn faith, and faith comes from God. Justification (the passage from sin to grace) is by faith alone and not by works, that is, not by morals or idealism in the daily life. This creed became the focal faith of Protestantism.

The Lotus Sutra, a Mahayana canon, says that people can be saved by faith alone (Watson 1993, p. 73). Cicero wrote:

> I am disposed to think that if reverence for gods were destroyed, we should also lose honesty and the brotherhood of mankind, and that most excellent of virtue, justice (Harbottle 1897, p. 81).

All living creatures, from the single cell of a bacterium to the 60 000 billion cells of a human being, are characterised by the desire to survive, both as an entity and a species, in any given environment. This comes from the instinct of self-preservation. And also since all the human societies the world over introduced the concept of deity as a means of survival, it is not hard to propose that all races throughout the history might have looked at the same supernatural existence with different eyes. All the peoples expressed gods, God, Heaven, Allah, Yahweh in their own way, and what they worshipped was in substance no different in the way they uttered the different languages but in reality meant the same thing. 'Kabir preached the notion of a monotheistic religion stripped of idols. In Kabir's teachings God was one, whether he was called Rama or Allah.' (Mercer 1996, p. 405)

The similarity of the moral codes or idealism around the world may be a surprise to anyone who ventured into the various idealistic cultures. I am going to illustrate that the peoples the world over had similar daily experiences and expressed their lessons learned in their own languages, pointing to the rule by the supernatural being.

The Buddha did not claim the originality of his doctrines. He repeated that he was following the ancient teachings developed by the saints and the awakened ones of the past. He was teaching the eternal truth, thus emphasising the universality of his messages. (Eliade 1982, p. 106)

'Heaven (or some references say God) helps those who help themselves' is a common proverb which came out from the accumulations of vast human experience. Though the maxim does not appear in the Bible, I am sure that the Christian theologians do not find much objection to it. Most of the people will agree with the massage it carries, by reflecting what they know from their life. Aeschylus wrote: When man hastens, God too works with him; God ever works with those who work with will (Harbottle 1897, p. 443). That matches with today's common notion that the more we put our mind into our work, the luckier we get. These passages carry virtually identical sense to the aforementioned proverb. This reasoning supports the proposition that gods, God, and Heaven are all the same in essence but people reasoned from the different perspectives.

The Russian saying that the gods blind those whom they want to destroy is similar to Greek passages by Lycurgus 'The gods do nothing until they have blinded the mind of the wicked' (p. 433), and by Aeschylus 'When 'tis God's will to bring an utter doom upon a house, He first in mortal men implants what works out' (p. 393), and also by Sophocles in

Antigone 'Whene'er, the deity misfortune plans for men, he first destroys his understanding' (p. 448). The following verse expresses the same message: When God will ruin He first deprives of his senses [Anon] (p. 279). The intent of these sayings is the opposite of those in the last paragraph.

The Manichaeans, the followers of the prophet Mani, practised a religion that combined elements of Zoroastrianism, Buddhism and Christianity (Oliphant 1992, p. 77).

The following verses have identical meanings. Work in thy youth thus shalt thrive in age [Menander] (Harbottle 1897, p. 424). Be sure no lie can ever reach old age [Sophocles] (p. 490). The last verse of Ecclesiastes goes: For God will bring every deed into judgement, including every hidden thing, whether it is good or evil (Ecclesiastes 12:14). If you gathered nothing in your youth, how can you find anything in your old age (Sirach 25:3)? They who have not led the holy life, who in youth have not acquired wealth, pine away like old herons at a pond without fish [a Buddhist cannon] (Narada 1993, p. 142). The mind is slow to unlearn what it learnt early [Seneca] (Harbottle 1897, p. 41). Our memory is naturally most tenacious of those things which we learn in our raw youth [Quintilian] (p. 41).

There is a Chinese saying: Heaven blesses those who do good but visits calamity upon wrong-doers (Chien 1979, p. 307). This saying has the identical message as the biblical message: If you follow God's precepts, you will reap a blessing, and if you don't you will reap a curse (e.g., Deuteronomy 30:15-18). King Shun said, 'He who humbles himself makes himself great' (Chien 1979, p. 66). Christ made the same statement, and similarly Aesop wrote, 'The proud shall be humbled and the humbled exalted' (Harbottle 1897, p. 499). Further, the avenging god follows in the steps of the proud [Seneca] (p. 264). The gods implore to crush the proud and elevate the poor [Horace] (p. 43). The punishment of pride and cruelty will be heavy though it may be long in coming [Livy] (p. 281). *The Dhammapada* reads, 'As sweet as honey is an evil deed, so thinks the fool so long as it ripens not; but when it ripens, then he comes to grief' (Narada 1993, p. 68).

The illustrations can go on. Hesiod wrote: Seek not dishonest gain; dishonest gains are losses (Harbottle 1897, p. 415). Antiphanes: Ill-gotten gains may some small pleasure give, but in the end bring untold misery (p. 416). Menander: All profit that is dishonest brings disaster (p. 416). Euripides: Ill-gotten gains are oftentimes changed to loss (p. 485). Sophocles: Gains ill-gotten by a godless fraud can never prosper (p. 497). Menander: Count gain as gain, if only it be honest (p. 510). Periander: Ill-gotten gains are a treasure that weighs us down (p. 415). Democritus: The hope of dishonest gain is the beginning of loss (p. 368). Chilo: Loss is to be preferred to discreditable gain, for one causes transient, the other lifelong sorrow (p. 382). Seneca: Wealth is a slave of a wise man, the master of a fool (p. 97). Seneca again: The wise man will never admit within his doors a penny of ill-gotten gains (p. 258). Pliny the Younger: Men are so enslaved by the lust of gain that they seem to be possessed by it, rather than possess it (p. 97). Plautus: There are many traps laid to ensnare mankind, and whosoever snaps at the bait is caught by his own greediness (p. 98). These passages have corresponding verses in the Bible:

> Treasures gained by wickedness do not profit, ... (Proverbs 10:2).
> Bread gained by deceit is sweet, but afterward the mouth will be full of gravel (Proverbs 20:17).

'Learn, being human, to control thy wrath' (Harbottle 1897, p. 329) by Menander, a classical Greek dramatist, carries the same message as 'Anger dwells in fools' (e.g., Proverbs 12:16, 14:29, 16:32, 29:11) of the Bible. *The Dhammapada*, a Buddhist cannon, goes:

> Whoso checks his up-risen anger as though it were a rolling chariot, him I call a true charioteer. Other charioteers are mere rein-holders. (Narada 1993, p. 190)

Dionysius Cato wrote:

> Anger so cloud the mind that it cannot perceive the truth (Harbottle 1897, p. 96).

Further, Menander wrote, 'Whatever man does in anger, be sure, will prove hereafter to be wrongly done' (p. 330).

Euripides' verse 'All things are born of earth; all things earth takes again' (p. 331) reminds us the biblical phrase 'from dust to dust'. Aesop wrote, 'Naked came into the world, and naked shall we depart from it' (p. 347). This statement is also similar to the familiar biblical verse.

The following Geek verses are similar in intent to the important teachings of the Old Testament:

- Anon: 'Tis by the fate ordained that all mankind from evil councils evil harvests reap (p. 362).
- Phocylides: If ill thou judge, God will judge thee after (p. 391).
- Sophocles: Take heart, my child, take heart; Mighty in heaven dwells, Zeus, who heholdeth and directeth all (p. 392).
- Homer: The gods know all things (p. 393).
- Phocylides: The spirit is the image of God, and his vehicle of communication with men (p. 481).
- Aeschylus: For the lips of Zeus know not to speak a lying speech, but will perform each single word (p. 535).
- A god indeed was he, most noble Memmius, who first laid down for us that rule of life which men call Wisdom [Lucretius] (p. 44).
- The fame which is based on wealth or beauty is a frail and fleeting thing; but virtue shines for ages with undiminished lustre [Sallust] (p. 49).
- God has no throne but earth and sea and air and sky and virtue. Why in more distant realms seek we the gods! Whate'er we feel or see is Jove himself. [Lucan] (p. 60)

Most of the people today ought to know how accurate the above passages and verses are upon reflecting their own experience. We think the Bible is religious and the Greek verses are philosophical but the above passages do not indicate they are any different.

Montaigne wrote:

> For myself, I prefer to believe that they [philosophers] treated knowledge [of man and wisdom] casually, like a toy to play around with, and amused themselves with reason as with a vain and frivolous instrument, putting forward all sorts of notions and fancies, sometimes more studied, sometimes more loose. This same Plato, who defines man as he would a chicken, says elsewhere, after Socrates, that in truth he does not know what man is, and that he is one part of the world as difficult as any to know. (Montaigne 1965, p. 408)

Polytheism pointed to the concept of various gods who had limited authority. These gods tended to be capricious and the central notion of the faith may be to appease the frivolous gods by sacrificing animals and humans. The people under polytheism tended, reflecting the limited authority of gods, to surrender only a part of their life to gods. Monotheism required one god to be omniscient and omnipotent. The people under this mode of religion often emphasised God who encourages the ethical life. Seriousness of the believers characterised monotheism, and the religion of this mode tended to embrace the whole life of the followers.

I wrote earlier that the material culture characterised the Egyptian civilisation. However, the largest portion of the surviving literature in Egypt is religious; not the religion of the individuals but of the state. The state machinery was also regarded as a religious institution designed to exalt and honour the gods through its head pharaoh. (Breasted 1950, pp. 455-6) Among the atmosphere of material civilisation of Egypt there were two pharaohs of note who genuinely cherished idealism.

Amenemhet I (2000-1970 BC) escaped with his life from the assassination attempt which nearly succeeded. This king, when old, told to his son, feeling bitter about an attempt on his life, that his son should not trust anyone and people took advantage of his being kind. (pp. 177-9)

Also the Egyptian pharaoh Akhenaton (1375-1358 BC), believing that there was only one god 'Aton', tried to compel his subjects to abandon their various deities, but failed (Davison 1993, p. 28). This religious revolution antagonised the priest class, particularly the Amon priests, and the general public. Amon was the god of Thebe and also spelled Amen or Amun. His insistence on peace also antagonised the army. The king composed two hymns to Aton, which are engraved on the walls of the tomb chapels. It is well known that the hymns bear remarkable similarities to a few verses in Psalm 104 of the Christian Bible. All life giving of Aton is replaced by all life giving of God of Judaism. (Breasted 1950, pp. 371-6)

Monotheism is the central theme of Judaeo-Christian-Islamic religion in defiance to the polytheism of the surrounding nations. The first of the Ten Commandments is: You shall have no other gods before me (Exodus 20:3). The author of the Decalogue was aware that the peoples around, for example, the Canaanites, had their own gods, and thus insisted the Jews adhere to Yahweh incorporating the above teaching into the Ten Commandments. The author and the Jews could not tolerate the idea that the gods and Yahweh might be the same god viewed by the different peoples. For them God was as taught in the Old Testament and no other. Interestingly, Baal, referred to as an epitome of evil in the Old Testament, means 'Lord' in Hebrew (Eliade 1978, p. 184). The Bible adopted the theme that the Jewish God was stronger than any other gods, for example, Baal, god of Phoenician and Canaanite lands. Thus the Jews achieved the conquest as the Bible narrates. There is a further twist to the theme. The Jews adopted a large part of Canaanite sacrificial system, though the Old Testament does not refer to this fact.

- The Jews regarded offering as food of the divinity (Judge 6:19).
- The Jews built sanctuaries after Canaanite models.
- Israelite ecstatic prophecy has its root in Canaanite religion.
- The Jews organised the priestly class after Canaanite models.

One of the five 'pillars', the basic commandments of Islam, is an utterance of faith 'I testify that there is no God but the God, and that Muhammad is the messenger of God'.

In the ancient to classical Greek world two systems of thoughts existed, that is, the anthropomorphism of the popular or state cults based on the Hesiodic pantheon, and the belief in the supreme divine force which is parallel to the divinity of Judaic tradition. The question of one god or many hardly troubled the ancient to classical Greeks. When Demosthenes wrote, 'Only the gods make no mistakes' (Harbottle 1897, p. 420), its message, similar to the Judaic tradition, hardly mattered if the gods had been expressed in a singular form.

Socrates freely talked about polytheism and monotheism, but it seems he believed in the Supreme Mind responsible for the ordering of the universe and the creation of men. He believed in God, omniscient and omnipotent, similar to that expressed in the Christian Bible. Plato did not bother to make distinctions. (Guthrie 1969, pp. 226-7, 476)

We modern people have a custom of saying that we are lucky when something favourable happens to us without much control from us; however, the ancient people had a custom of saying that gods were with them when similar happening occurred to them. Aesop expressed the idea in the verse: The earth is sometimes a mother, and sometimes a step-mother (Harbottle 1897, p. 385). The familiar English word 'good' is of Germanic origin meaning 'god' reflecting religious thinking.

Monotheism is conducive to the omnipotence of God, whereas polytheism defines and limits the power of each god. Generally people who believed in One Supreme Being with subsequent qualities felt superior to the people who believed in many gods, which became the driving force of their zeal for conquest and conversion.

Divinity may be conceived either singular or plural. The former emphasises the unifying force of the various manifestations and the latter the separate forces of the universal plan. The modern world looks askance at the elaborate pantheons of the Greeks, Egyptians and Hindus. (Hall 1984, p. 28)

Buddhism in its essence stresses constant effort rather than faith, to reach the enlightened state of nirvana. However, some sects, notably Amida sect, place emphasis on the premise that people can be saved only through faith. The teachings of these sects often delude us into thinking that the message of the canons is no different from that of the Bible, especially that of Psalms. The above Buddhist sects tell their followers that an individual cannot attain nirvana unless aided by the vows of the Buddha who in this context refers to a historical person Gautama Siddhartha. However, here again, I don't see any difference in reality if we replace the word Gautama by such terms as the Buddha, gods, God, or Heaven. This concept has a parallel in Christian teaching: Christ's crucifixion is interpreted as redemption of sins by his followers; the followers are delivered from punishment through suffering of Christ. *The Lankavatara Sutra* insists on the striving efforts by the followers but at the same time emphasises the Buddha's power aids the followers. Without these assistances, the followers would never be able to lead to the enlightenment. (*The Lankavatara Sutra* 1932, p. xiii)

The above line of argument may infuriate some Judaic, Christian and Islamic adherents. For these followers, God is omniscient and omnipotent and they recognise God only as presented by their scriptures. Any other forms of faith are utterly repugnant to them.

As I understand the Bible, to read the text literally in some parts, especially concerning creation of the world and humans, and some parts of history, is wrong. We should rely on the modern expert historians to get the accurate pictures of what really happened in the past. The authors of the Bible in the ancient Levant, in the absence of accurate knowledge, wrote the stories as best they could using the information available at the time. They could have made the factual narrations, stretched their imaginations to fill the gaps in the available information or concocted tales to promote their beliefs. The biblical history was an idealised narration based on the data available to the authors at the time. For example, the Book of Joshua deviates considerably from the historical evidence. Also the archaeological evidence does not support the story of Exodus where a large number of the Jews--600 000 men besides women and children according to Exodus 12:37--journeyed from Egypt to the Levant, though it was possible if there had been only a small number of them involved.

The scholars generally reject the historicity of the Exodus because of lack of archaeological evidence. However, I came upon the following video presenting the archaeological evidence: The Exodus Revealed - Startling Evidence for the Hebrew Exodus from Egypt.

Interestingly the Bible is not consistent about the values of faith and action. Some books say people can be saved only through faith: the others say only through actions, that is, their conduct of daily life. For instance, the Book of Romans expressly states that people will be saved only by faith which in turn promotes grace and mercy of God, and not by good works or deeds because all the people are sinners after all (Romans 3:21-8). A devout Christian uttered the following verses:

> Why will you put off your resolution from day to day? Arise, and begin this very instant, and say: Now is the time to do; now is the time to fight; now is the proper time to amend your life. (Thomas A Kempis 1982, p. 79)

The Council of Trent of 1546 debated the thorny question of justification by faith. There were divisions among the members. Some argued that men received grace by their own efforts and good works. Some argued that men received grace, as Luther maintained, by faith alone. (Mercer 1996, p. 437) Luther believed that men cannot be justified by their own works but only by the faith. Like faith, God accords salvation gratuitously. He firmly believed that God judges, condemns and saves according to God's own design. Hence he condemned *The Ethics* of Aristotle which expounded that education secures the moral virtues. Luther again insisted that good life have nothing to do with salvation. He incidentally thought that hymns chanted were important in the course of the service. (Eliade 1985, pp. 239-42)

St Augustine wrote many centuries earlier, "There was no salvation without divine grace and this could not necessarily be gained through living a 'good' life" (Freeman 1996, p. 515).

I don't think some inconsistencies and inaccuracies in the Bible diminish its high worth, as long as we maintain the critical mind over the message. We should read some of its stories, for example the story of Samson (Judges chs 13-16), with the same attitude as with the fairy tales, Greek mythology or Aesop's Fables, and not to be taken literally. The authors of these tales conjured up the stories as they saw fit without any inhibitions as the comic writers of the present day do. The results are products of imagination rather than those of pains-taking researches such as required for this series of books. We should try to enjoy and learn what is important for us.

We have to read the Bible for the sake of finding something useful for us in the same way we read any other books, picking up what we need. This approach is efficient and suitable for busy modern life. We should absorb only what we think is useful and discard the rest, though many Christian scholars may object to this approach.

Karl Marx believed that the evangelical stories in the Bible were all fabricated and did not entertain any other thoughts. As he claimed, the Bible contained some passages that hinted they were fabrications. There are also some teachings that are not acceptable to us. I enumerate the punishments for the breaches of the various ordinances in the next section. We cannot enforce most of these penalties in the modern society. We must adhere to the scientific creation theory, and the biblical creation is the artistic expressions of what the authors imagined happened in the past in the absence of accurate knowledge. 'The biblical story of the creation of the world and of Adam and Eve and the Serpent was also an ancient Babylonian story, and probably a still earlier Sumerian story.' (Wells 1925, p. 615) The evolution theory of Charles Darwin would not disturb people with the right attitude to Christianity.

We have to understand that the ancient people were generally illiterate and ignorant, and consequently the biblical authors had to present the teachings as they did. Even today many children's stories are receptive only to the kids and not to the adults. The Gospel According to Matthew opens with the genealogies of Jesus Christ. It states that Christ was descended from Abraham through David and Solomon. However, the same chapter one states that Joseph, supposedly Christ's father, did not consummate the marriage with Mary before Christ was born. It seems the author of the Gospel did not see any logical absurdity in the narration (p. 323), which, when pointed out, the author, as well as the modern readers, should be able to understand. Besides it strikes me quite odd that how the author got to know convincingly Mary was a virgin when she delivered Christ.

St Augustine believed in Manichaeism when young but after converting to Christianity--after 9 years, he rejected Manichaeism claiming that this religion was totally false (St Augustine 1907, p. 50).

When Augustine was 32 years of age, he converted to a true Christian (p. 148). During the severe struggle, he heard children from the neighbouring house singing and they sounded to him 'Take up and read! Take up and read!'. He interpreted it as the voice of God telling him to read the Scripture. He opened the Holy Book randomly and read the following passage and all his doubts instantly vanished:

> Not in rioting and drunkenness, not in chambering and wantonness, not in strife and envying; but put ye on the Lord Jesus Christ, and make not provision for flesh (p. 170).

'For hunger and thirst are in a manner pains; they burn and kill like a fever, unless the medicine of nourishments come to our aid.' After enlightenment, he still could not remove the sense of pleasure in eating and drinking and he had to fight it out every day. Augustine thought that his tears were acceptable sacrifice to God, not using words but sincere supplications: For what is nearer to Thine ears than a confessing heart, and a life of faith? He wrote that the friendship of this world is fornication against God. (pp. 13, 23, 231) He was referring to both friends and worldly affairs.

> Wretched is every soul bound by the friendship of perishable things; he is torn asunder when he loses them … (p. 57).
>
> Is not the life of man upon earth all trial? Thou are the physician, I sick; thou merciful, I miserable. (p. 228)
>
> But the natural man, as it were, a babe in Christ and fed on milk, until he be strengthened for solid meat (p. 326).

In fact, Saint Augustine (354-430), a great Christian theologian, accepted Christianity only after he was assured that he did not have to believe all the Bible stories literally. He was not a systematic theologian and many of his thoughts were response to the appeals from the Christians regarding the religious controversies. The essence of the Bible lies in spirit and not in inconsistencies, inaccuracies or material objects. He persistently denied the claim that the origin of evil should be sought in material objects.

I am to cite further an example of inconsistency of the Bible. God is omnipresent apart from being omniscient and omnipotent. Why then did God ask the Israelites to build a sanctuary (material objects) for God to live in (Exodus 25:8; 2 Samuel 5:6)? In the Book of Exodus God was referring to a tabernacle and in the Book of 2 Samuel God was referring to a temple. God, being omnipresent, does not need a place to live in. However, the later author of the Bible noticed and wrote about the absurdity of the request (Acts 7:48), thus condemning the material existence.

> Lo are they not full of their old leaven, who say to us, 'What was God doing before He made heaven and earth?' For if (say they) He was unemployed and wrought not, why does He not also henceforth and forever as He did heretofore? (St Augustine 1907, p. 259)

St Augustine understood that heaven and earth included all creatures and he did not know the answer to the above query.

He wrote *The City of God* (5th century) in Latin, the famous masterpiece. The book contrasts the Christians living in the city of God and the pagans living in the city of the world. The former will gain eternal salvation, the latter eternal punishment. The book also espouses the problematic concept of *predestination* which says that God chooses only certain individuals for salvation from God's freely given grace, that is, God predestinates some people for salvation.

The words Jesus Christ uttered when he was told to look at the magnificent temple clearly reveal the basic attitude of the Bible: Not one stone here will be left on another; everyone will be thrown down (Matthew 24:2).

Chapter 2 Judaism-Christianity-Islam

Section 1 Quiddity of Judaism-Christianity-Islam

Quiddity means that which makes what it is. I could not find a better word than this philosophical word to express my intent.

Formation of Old Testament

In spite of the fact that the Old Testament became the basis of the New Testament; and also the Bible (the Old and New Testaments), that of the Qur'an, the people do not agree how and when the Old Testament was written down.

The Old Testament, especially Exodus and Deuteronomy, shows the influence of the Code of Hammurabi, the laws the Babylonian ruler (d. c. 1750 BC) promulgated. More generally in the second millennium before the Indo-European invasions of 1500-1100 BC from the Eurasian Steppes, there was a cultural unity in the eastern Mediterranean. Comparisons of Homer's text, the first books of the Old Testament, and the epic poems from Egypt and Mesopotamia reveal unmistakable resemblances. (Rietbergen 1998, pp. 14, 22)

Traditionally the Jewish people regarded that Moses wrote the Torah or Pentateuch. The first five books of the Old Testament are often referred to as the Torah or Pentateuch, and consist of Genesis, Exodus, Leviticus, Numbers and Deuteronomy. These are the keys to understanding the Bible. It is conjectured that he wrote them in the Hebrew language during the exodus which lasted from c. 1446 to c. 1406 BC. Even we concede to the above notion, we must answer rather difficult questions.

In view of the written language it poses no problems. The Old Testament states that God handed down the two tablets of the Testimony the fingers of God inscribed at Sinai (Exodus 31:18). Moses smashed the two tablets into pieces when he saw the people made the golden calf and dancing (Exodus 32:19). He placed the two tablets in the ark (to be known as Ark of the Covenant) and placed the ark inside the tabernacle (Exodus 40:20): He had written the words of the covenant--the Ten Commandments--on these tablets by the Lord's command (Exodus 34:28). Research shows that the Semitic people in Syria and Palestine knew how to express their speech in an alphabetical writing by about 1500 BC, modifying Egyptian hieroglyphics.

There are a few problems. The narration of the Bible starts at c. 2500 BC and Moses had to rely on the oral traditions (stories, poems and proverbs) to cover the history stretching as long as 1000 years. Was any one person capable of writing such literary, historical and religious books; creative, imaginative yet detailed in many parts? even we ascribe a superhuman capability to Moses. The last chapter of Deuteronomy describes how Moses died, which he could not have written. It is widely recognised that the interpolations were carried out not only of the Torah but of the other books of the Old Testament to suit the new information available.

Some scholars believe that the Pentateuch passed down orally until being written down between 1000 BC and 400 BC: The major works were done during the reigns of King David (1010-970 BC) and King Solomon (970-930 BC).

It is naturally expected that as the time went on the authorship of the books in the Old Testament became clearer. For example, the prophets bearing the same names respectively were thought to have written down the books of Isaiah (chs 1-39) and Jeremiah. Some scholars believe that Isaiah wrote the rest of the book (chs 40-66) in his late years, whereas some scholars believe that Deutero-Isaiah (another prophet) wrote these chapters. Isaiah, son of Amoz, was a major Hebrew prophet of Judah in the 8th century BC. Jeremiah was also a major Hebrew prophet of Judah and lived c. 650-c. 585 BC.

Whatever authorship we ascribe to the Old Testament, it has only a secondary importance. What is written in the Testament, provided it is true to our thinking and experience, is paramount to us.

Going through the Christian Bible many times, a strong notion caught my mind. The Holy Scripture says God will punish us if we do not follow his precepts. In the Old Testament the punishments to the breaches of some ordinances are so severe to the extreme that they are virtually unworkable. For example:

- Whoever curses father or mother shall be put to death (Exodus 21:17).
- Any person who profanes Sabbath must be put to death (Exodus 31:14).
- Whoever kidnaps a person whether that person has been sold or still in possession, shall be put to death (Exodus 21:16).
- Whoever sacrifices to any god, other than the Lord alone, shall be devoted to destruction (Exodus 22:20).
- A young woman who is not a virgin at the wedding night shall be stoned to death (Deuteronomy 22:20-1).
- Adulterers, both the man and the woman, shall be put to death (Deuteronomy 22:22).

The Bible upholders meted out the draconian penalties at times, but if they had carried out the penalty to the letter at every breach, they would not have left many people alive. However, the Bible does not specify the degree of punishments to the breaches of many precepts. This is particularly true in the New Testament. For instance, the New Testament does not even say what penalties would be administered to the common criminal acts of murder or theft, though the Old Testament specifies the penalties for these crimes. The criminal laws of the present day would impose heavy sentence for murder and light sentence for theft. However, the New Testament does not show any degrees of punishments for the transgression of the precepts but uniformly condemn them in a qualitative term. The punishments in the Old Testament above mentioned are more figurative than actual.

In contradistinction with the Bible, the Qur'an (Koran) often gives out a practical penalty for a certain sin or crime. For example, the Qur'an prescribes the following punishment for adultery:

> The adulteress and adulterer flog each of them a hundred stripes, and let not pity for them detain you from obedience to Allah, if you believe in Allah and the Last Day, and let a party of believers witness their chastisement (Qur'an 24.2).

Since I became familiar with the Bible, I tried to follow its precepts as much as I could. However, I did not or more precisely could not adhere to some ordinances, particularly honour my parents, do not commit adultery and leave the revenge to God. There is nothing strange that I could not observe some precepts from various reasons. What strikes me most is that in spite of my neglect on some matters God granted me everything what I wished for. I even got what I wished in my recess of my mind. Certainly I was punished for the repeated wrong thinking and conducts with a good reason. When I say everything, it did not include fabulous wealth and sex since they are not what God wanted me to have. I acquired wealth to live my life comfortably, and developed sexual laws in Book Five to guide my sexual longing. Wealth and sex have more to do with pleasure and not much to do with God (Truth). The above line of thinking leads me to a few possibilities as to why I was blessed in spite of my serious neglect on some of the God's laws.

Sexual activities may be akin to eating and drinking in that they all satisfy the need of the body. Men want food and drinks and women. Sins as the Bible describes concerning the immoral sexual activities may be no worse that the strong longing for food and drinks. Hence we may not be punished for the sexual sins though the Bible says we would.

I got another idea. Rewards and punishments in the God's laws may be working on the 'majority principle'. It is true I did not carry out all what the Bible urges us to do; however, I was quite careful to follow the other ordinances which formed in fact a majority in terms of number. I passed the examination God set, not by 100 per cent but with some margin. Hence God granted me what I asked for: recovery of my health and acquisition of good qualifications; and even gave me opportunities to see many of my enemies ruined though wishing the destruction of the enemies is against the biblical teaching.

The biblical scholars may insist that the above events happened because God is merciful and trying to teach us to be merciful and tolerant to other people. This is the repeatedly expressed position of the Bible. For instance, the Book of Ezra has the following passage:

> After all that has come upon us for our evil deeds and for our great guilt, seeing that you, our God, have punished us less than our iniquities deserved and have given us such a remnant as this, ... (Ezra 9:13).

I have come up with another possible interpretation, which, I have come to believe, is closest to the truth. The morals which are parts of statutes, ordinances or precepts may not be the focal point of the biblical teachings, and the essence of the Scripture may lie somewhere else. The morals are human conducts mainly directed to the fellow human beings. Breaches of the moral laws may not in themselves bring about the punishment. Also the same breach in one person may not result in the same punishment in another. The ethical conducts the Ten Commandments represent may be periphery to the God's teachings. When Jesus Christ was asked which commandment in the law was the greatest, he said, 'You shall love the Lord your God with all your heart, and with all your soul, and with all your mind' (Matthew 22:37). This verse in fact runs through the Old and New Testaments like the backbone, with some phrases altered at times. 'For the love of God is this, that we obey his commandments. And his commandments are not burdensome, for whatever is born of God conquers the world.' (1 John 5:3-4) The author gives out his understanding of the term in a concrete form, though I suspect that love of God means a lot more than obeying his commandments; in a similar manner to love someone in the human relations means a lot more than obeying the wishes of that person. If love of God is only obeying the commandments of God, we can equate 'Love thy neighbour' to love of God and the argument becomes circular and do not define what to love God entails. The Bible also expresses love of God in the opposite form of fear of God. For example, it says: Fear the Lord your God, serve him only and take the oaths in his name (Deuteronomy 6:13).

> It is evident that no one is justified before God by the law; for 'The one who is righteous will live by faith' (Galatians 3:11).

The law means the Law of Moses or the morals. The faith works through love. If you live by faith, you are not subject to the law. (Galatians 3:15-25)

Democritus, an ancient Greek, wrote, 'Those only are lovers of the gods who hate injustice' (Harbottle 1897, p. 423). In this verse he equates love of the gods with carrying out justice. According to the Bible, love of God entails to carry out what is right and just in the society, whether people are happy or not, whether the judgments suit the people concerned or not. The Bible and the Buddhist cannons are not the discourses as to how to be happy, and are beyond the emotional plane. This commandment referring to love of God is also the central teaching of Islam and expressed as submission to Allah.

God of the Jews, the Christians and the Muslims is omniscient and omnipotent. For Jeremiah God was ultimate. We can find this concept in the ancient Greek thoughts. Anonymous ancient Greek wrote, 'The eye of Zeus sleeps not, and, though far off, is ever near' (p. 470). Wherefore conceal thou nothing. Time that sees and hears all things bringeth all to light [Sophocles]. (p. 490) Time brings the truth to light [Menander] (p. 490). Contrary to the general view of Christianity, St Augustine was convinced after studying Neo-Platonism that God was present in the soul of every human being.

> The basis of Luther's faith was not the authority of the Bible; it was his own experience, which he there found confirmed but naturally he was forced to turn more and more to the authority in disputes with others. However, he never regarded it as infallible, and constantly used the Gospel as the criterion of what in it was and what was not true. Belief, like the moral life, is a fruit of faith, not its essence. (Randall 1976, p. 150)

The pharaoh in the ancient Egypt is the incarnation of order. This order can be equated with God, truth, light and justice; Jesus Christ identified himself to these qualities. In the texts of different origins and periods in Egypt there are such declarations as these:

- Incite your heart to know order.
- I make thee to know the thing of order in your heart; mayest thou do what is right for thee!
- I was a man who loved order and hated sin. For I know that sin is an abomination to God.

(Eliade 1978, p. 91)

The ways of salvation according to Hinduism incredibly include the above commandment:

- the way of action; good works including sacrifices
- the way of knowledge
- the way of the love of God; dividing into human's love to God and God's love to humans

(Kung et al. 1986, p. 218)

> The individual person is the sacrificial animal; his attachments to the cycle of existence are the fetters. Only someone who devoutly sacrifices himself as it were, by completely surrendering to the Lord Shiva achieves salvation. (p. 222)
>
> Hindus believe in not only the continuity of the individuals through many lives, but also in a cyclical course of history, in which worlds arise, gradually move towards their downfall, and are created anew. ... the fulfilment of human life: liberation through entrance into 'nirvana' or the 'Kingdom of God'. (p. 237)

Christ reiterates the importance of the aforementioned verse 'Love of God' by belittling the other commandments in various occasions. 'Honour your parents' is an important precept in the Bible. Still he said, 'Whoever loves father or mother more than me is not worthy of me; and whoever loves son or daughter more than me is not worthy of me, ...' (Matthew 10:37). In the Old Testament, Abraham was prepared to kill his beloved son without hesitation or questioning the motives of God, when God commanded him to sacrifice his son. Morally, murdering his only son must have been a heinous crime; emotionally, losing his son must have been an unbearable bereavement under any other circumstances. The Bible, here also, clearly indicates that God's commands should override every other considerations, such as morals or families.

As the consequence of the above disclosures, the statute 'Love one another' among the biblical teachings may not be as important as some Christians are led to believe, although the following verse stresses the importance of love: Whoever does not love does not know God, for God is love (1 John 4:8). The Bible (Matthew 22:39) says that this statute is second in importance and the morals flow out of it. Rudimentary sense of morals observed at times among animals does not come from the concept of 'Love thy neighbour' but comes from instincts. The last paragraph says that the faithful can break the ethics in reverence to the cardinal teaching. This interpretation matches with the following verse from the Old Testament: If a person sins against another, someone can intercede for the sinner with the Lord; but if someone sins against the Lord, who can make intercession (1 Samuel 2:25)? Many non-Christian philosophers reached to a conclusion that the morals are not that important in establishing the absolute truth. In the ancient to classical Greek cities, 'Love thy neighbour' strongly manifested as the search for justice among the Greek men.

A mendicant who lives alone in the forest cannot practise the concept of 'Love thy neighbour'; however, he still can follow the teaching 'Love your God'. This may be one indication of the biblical message that the latter is more fundamental than the former.

According to Genesis, God made humans in the likeness of God (Genesis 1:26). This verse and the others may give erroneous interpretations of God. God talks humans using the human language, which also gives a wrong impression of God. The authors had to present the Bible in the way they did for the sheer necessity to communicating with the general public who were mostly illiterate and ignorant. I believe God does not have a human shape and does not communicate with us using language.

Possibly God is beyond the considerations of time and space, though for us humans it is impossible to gauge the life and existence without these concepts. Heaven and hell as we conceive are valid only when we remove time and space frames. St Augustine asks the following questions. Did God create time and space when he made heaven and earth? What was God doing before he made heaven and earth? (St Augustine 1907, pp. 259-62)

The heaven and hell after death depending on the moral standards while alive have a few critical flaws. What happens to the babies who die? Do they all go to heaven? What happens to the majority of people who are neither good nor evil to the extreme? Where is the abode of heaven and hell? Is there any time limit in heaven and hell?

The biblical explanation of the creation of the world and humans was the author's imaginations in the absence of the data of the actual creation. It ignored the time and space considerations and was a lot easier than explaining the actual event. The evolution theory is correct and the creation theory as the Bible presents gives us a wrong idea of God unless we are careful. The modern scientists are trying to explain the creation of the universe not only by observations and analyses but by imaginations.

The New Testament gives important clues refuting the anthropomorphic presentation of God in the Old Testament. Jesus said, 'I am the light of the world' (John 8:12), and also said, 'I am the way, and the truth, and the life' (John 14:6). The Old Testament also says: And now, O Lord God, you are God, and your words are true, and you have promised this good thing to your servant (2 Samuel 7:28). If we equate God to the above abstract words instead of giving God the human shape, we are in a better position to understanding the Bible. God is an immutable law of nature which nobody can escape, whether they are Christians or Buddhists. 'God is dead.' 'God cannot die. God cannot go back on his words. God cannot do this or that.' (Montaigne 1965, p. 392) These remarks stem from a wrong concept of God. If truth sets you free, you are truly free, and need care nothing for the vain words of men (Thomas A Kempis 1952, p. 95). What are words but words only? They fly to and fro but hurt not so much as a stone. (p. 153) My son, if your peace depends on anyone, by reason of your affection or friendship with him, you will always be unsettled, and dependent on him.

But if you turn to the living and eternal Truth, the departure or death of your friend will not distress you. (p. 148) Also the same author wrote: All human comfort is short-lived and empty; but blessed and true is the comfort received inwardly from the Truth (p. 114). To whom shall I give credit, Lord? to whom but to thee? Thou art the Truth, which neither doth deceive, nor can be deceived. (Thomas a Kempis 1980, p. 225) For love of God, cheerfully endure everything—labour, sorrow, temptation, provocation, anxiety, necessity, weakness, injury and insult; censure, humiliation, disgrace, contradiction and contempt (Thomas A Kempis 1952, p. 141). The author, a pious Christian, in the above passages, virtually equates God with Truth.

The first of the Ten Commandments expresses the basic tenet of the Bible: You shall have no other gods before me. Also the Bible (Exodus 20:4) gives out the following prohibition in the second of the Ten Commandments:

> You shall not make yourself an idol, whether in the form of anything that is in heaven above, or that is on the earth beneath, or that is in the water under the earth.

In the history of Judaism, Christianity and Islam, aniconism and iconoclasm were often the subjects of controversy. Aniconism is opposition to making icons or images representing living creatures or divinities. Iconoclasm is destruction of icons and religious images.

The Qur'an places a strict prohibition on idolatry and polytheism (e.g., 10.66; 98.6; 29.25; 31.13). The first pillar of Islam well expresses the idea: I bear witness that there is no God but Allah and I bear witness that Muhammad is the Messenger of Allah. In Islam there are two considerations fused together:

- the absolute prohibition on idolatry and polytheism,
- the prohibition of making the pictorial representation of living things, since this may lead to the pictorial representation of God and people may worship them.

From about the middle of the 8th century the second prohibition became the standard thought but its applicability was somewhat modified.

It is also interesting to note that in the early Buddhism the Buddha was not represented iconically.

The Greek philosophy deals with wisdom which focuses on truth, justice and beauty: the Bible deals with love which focuses on truth and justice. The Greeks looked at truth, justice and beauty from the viewpoint of wisdom: the Jews looked at truth and justice from the viewpoint of love. The Qur'an also stands on a similar premise:

> Supremely exalted is Allah, the King, the Truth (Qur'an 20.114); This is because Allah is the Truth, and that which they call upon besides him is falsehood, and that Allah is the High, the Great (Qur'an 31.30). What cause can we have not to believe in God and the truth which has come to us, seeing that we long for our Lord to admit us to the company of the righteous? (Qur'an 5.84)

Montaigne wrote:

> The first stage in the corruption of morals is the banishment of truth: for, as Pindar said, to be truthful is the beginning of a great virtue, and is the first article that Plato required in the governor of his republic (Montaigne 1965, p. 505).

The Dhammapada offers the following verses:

The gift of truth excels all (other) gifts. The flavour of truth excels all (other) flavours. The pleasure in truth excels all (other) pleasures. (Narada 1993, p. 270)

In fact if we equate God with Truth we can overcome the various difficulties:

- This interpretation eliminates the nonsensical arguments in the Bible such as the concepts of resurrection of Christ, trinity, Virgin Mary, the biblical creation theory and the geocentric notion. Further this interpretation nullifies the rather silly arguments. God should not punish any bodies for their sins because God is love and also if God is omniscient, God should know when a person is born if it is good or bad. These arguments gave rise to the birth of theodicy which tries to justify the good and justice of God in the presence of evils in the world. One flaw coming from the establishment of all mighty God is that people ask questions such as why then God does not lead people to perfect virtue or why God cannot see the future. People ask this kind of questions because people misunderstand the concept of God.
- We do not have to be worried about heaven and hell; angels and devils, after life. I am a religious person but I don't believe in afterlife.
- The biblical prohibition of making idols of God makes sense if we equate God with truth. Philemon, an ancient Greek, well wrote: No painter and no sculptor, by the gods!, can carve or limn a form so beautiful as truth possesses (Harbottle 1897, p. 465). Do not make idolatry. Do not draw the picture of God; do not sculpt the shape of God. These prohibitions naturally follow from the logical premise that god (truth) cannot be given any human shape and we cannot do obeisance to god (truth). There is a conception, a prejudice in our minds such that when a man thinks of God, a human form occurs to us [Cicero] (Montaigne 1965, p. 397).
- If we equate God to truth, the statements that people believe in God or not, or God exists or not are nonsensical since truth is there irrespective. Hermes Trismegistos wrote that truth is the extreme manifestation of virtue (p. 384). These things clearly proclaim the power of nature, that which we call God [Pliny the Elder] (p. 208). Whether people read the Bible or not, whether they believe in its teachings or not, they get the same result. If they live in accordance with the teachings from whatever sources they have the ideas; from the Bible, from the other books or from their innate feelings, they have the rewards individually and as a group as the Bible describes. If they don't they reap the punishments.
- God = truth, Daoism = truth, Buddhism = truth, Judaism = truth, Christianity = truth, Islam = truth, Confucianism = truth, since all the adherents believe their teaching is the truth. This line of argument also promotes harmony and tolerance towards people of the other religions, whether they live separately or together. We get the impression that in the long past the people of the different religions lived separated by nations or by regions; however, they tend to live next doors nowadays. Hence the tolerance may be more important today than in the past.
- The Qur'an supports this interpretation:

> And for every nation there is a messenger. So when their messenger comes, the matter is decided between them with justice, and they are not wronged. (Qur'an 10.47)
>
> And certainly we raised in every nation a messenger, saying: Serve Allah [Truth] and shun the devil. Then of them was he whom Allah guided, and of them was he whose remaining in error was justly due. So travel in the land, then see what was the end of the rejecters. (Qur'an 16.36)

- We can equate the Kingdom of God of the Bible with the Kingdom of Truth, which we can again equate with nirvana of Buddhism. Jesus said, '… the Kingdom of God is within you' (Luke 17:21), and '… the Kingdom of God is of righteousness, peace and joy in the Holy Spirit …' (Romans 14:17).
- Love of God is hard to understand if we give God the human image; but love of the light, the way, the truth and the life makes good sense.
- This understanding is compatible with the present day of scientific and technical dominance.
- This interpretation gives us a broader perspective in the world religions. The doctrines taught by the multitudes of buddhas, passed down in oral and written forms, are called the dharma. This dharma means truth or law or the universal cosmic law. (Lopez 1996, p. 16)
- God is truth. We can interpret 'Do not serve the other gods' as meaning that people should serve the truth only and do not go after low desires such as wealth, sex, honour and fame. The above thinking answers the query why God does not grant happiness and fairness in regard with the above desires to all the moral and just people.
- When Christ preached, 'The time is fulfilled, and the Kingdom of God has come near; repent, and believe in the good news' (Mark 1:15), some Jews understood it meaning that the independent Jewish kingdom is at hand to be delivered from the Roman rule. The Muslims understood the advent of the Kingdom of God as meaning the coming of the Prophet (Muhammad). If we equate God to truth, there can be only one interpretation, that is, the spiritual release for the individual and the community.
- If God is truth, how can we explain the reward and the punishment for the moral existence? The reward and punishment do not come from a supreme being but from the truth. I have found that as the time goes on we get to know the truth of any matter, that is, the truth reveals itself as long as we keep seeking the truth earnestly.

The above interpretation may go against the conventional interpretation of the Bible and the Qur'an. It hints that some followers of these religions misunderstood the message. It also mocks and nullifies many of the historical happenings in regard to religion.

During an intimate conversation with a prostitute where we lay naked in a bed, I happened to mention I had a love doll--a female torso without limbs and a head. She quipped that a female head was something to hang onto in lovemaking. I have come to believe that the concept of God is something people hang onto in dealing with truth and reward and retribution. God is a lever the people use to look into the deeper insight in regard to the laws of life and the world.

Gandhi, after studying the New Testament and *The Gita*, realised the similar message and further postulated the unity of all religions. He saw love as the centre of all religions as both Christ and Krishna emphasised love as the basis of human existence. (Koller 1985, p. 119)

> For Gandhi, Truth is the God that dwells in all beings, and love is the soul-force by which they move. Through love, God or Truth is revealed (p. 121). Also the Bible says: … the Holy Spirit who lives in us (2 Timothy 1:14); … the truth, which lives in us and will be with us forever (2 John 1:2).

Gandhi, through up-bringing in the Jaina community, learned two maxims as two lessons in life:

> 'There is nothing higher than truth' was a wisdom taught in the Rig Veda, where the normative functioning of existence is regarded as its truth. 'Non-hurting or love is the highest virtue' is also a moral wisdom that has shaped the Indian tradition for thousands

of years. (Koller 1985, p. 119)

Mahatma Gandhi, himself a devout Hindu, attempted wholeheartedly to end the feud between the Hindus and the Muslims; however, as the result the fanatics of both religions hated him, and a Hindu extremist assassinated him. Mahatma means Great Soul.

God (Truth) granted me everything what I wanted and also showed me the destruction of many of my enemies, since I was observant of the most important commandment in spite of the fact I was deficient in lesser ordinances. When I said everything, naturally it did not include wealth and sex. Possibly committing a crime itself is not a sin, but going against the commandments of God (Truth) is a sin against God (Truth). Hence God (Truth), when perceived so, delivers punishments on the offenders, whose modes are not necessarily in the way humans judge.

My financial status made me lead a comfortable life and I could devote to writing books not being worried about money. I had a lot of sexual problems since puberty and I wrote Book Five *The Sexual Laws* in an effort to overcome the difficulties. If I had become fabulously rich and obtained sex easily, I would have become arrogant and forgotten about God (Truth) and would not have bothered to write books. Instead I would have indulged in drinks, gambling and sex, which, I must confess, still fascinate me in my old age.

Thus, the essence of the Bible may be the relationship between God (Truth) and us, and that relation decides our fate, irrespective of how observant we are concerning the other fellow humans or by what we call the morals. According to the New Testament, by the redemption of Jesus Christ, the believers can be saved even though they commit sins going against the Law of Moses. That is, we are judged according to how close we get to the cardinal teaching rather than our individual acts. Humble St Francis well expressed this observation when he said, ‘For what everyone is in thy sight, that is he, and no more’ (Thomas a Kempis 1980, p. 245). Pascal believed that true faith will appear only in the morally right.

True Christians as for true Buddhists are prepared to discard even families and friends, not to mention wealth and sex, to be close to truth. Both adherents will try to attain godliness and to avoid worldliness at every occasion.

> They [the Saints] renounced all riches, dignities, honours, friends and kindred; they desired to possess nothing in this world (Thomas A Kempis 1952, p. 46). Who is freer than he who desires nothing upon earth (p. 135)? God with His Holy angels will draw near to him who withdraws himself from his friends and acquaintances (p. 52). For Our Lord bestows His blessings where He finds vessels empty to receive them. The more completely a man renounces the worldly things, and the more perfectly he dies to self by the conquest of self, the sooner will grace be given, the more richly will he be infused, and nearer to God will he raise the heart set free from the world. (p. 212)
>
> That which is made of iron, wood or hemp, is not a strong bond, say the wise; the longing for jewels, ornaments, children and wives is a far greater attachment. That bond is strong, say the wise: It hurls down, is supple, and is hard to loosen. This too the wise cut off, and leave the world, with no longing, renouncing sensual pleasures. [a Buddhist canon] (Narada 1993, p. 265)

The Qur’an (Qur’an 3.14) says: But in nearness to God is the best of the goals (to return to).

Equals, as the proverb says, delight in equals [Plato] (Harbottle 1897, p. 400). This verse is an observation rather than an ethical teaching.

An ancient Greek wrote that what matters to us is outwardly friends and inwardly intelligence. The ultimate Christian theology as for the Buddhist doctrines denies even friends and intelligence for the true believers and urges people to empty their minds of all the worldly affairs such that God (Truth) comes and lives with them. In this context, friends and intelligence are not the truth. Xenophon wrote, 'To want nothing is god like, and the less we want the nearer we approach to the divine' (p. 511).

If we keep away from the low desires, we are close to God (Truth). When we are having pleasure, we are away from God (Truth). Hence while we are intoxicated, or under the urge for gambling, sex or narcotics, we tend to err in our judgement. Christianity as for Buddhism prohibits even gazing women with sexual intent; this is most likely because men are indulging in pleasure though brief and seemingly innocent. '… for I, the Lord your God, am a jealous God ….' (Exodus 20:5) Accordingly God delivers punishment when we pay attention to something other than God (Truth). When we are suffering we are close to God (Truth). When I suffered in my youth wondering if the life is worth living, though I did not even know the concept of God at the time God (Truth) was in fact the closest to me.

> When you think I am far away, then often I am nearest to you (Thomas A Kempis 1952, p. 134).

Closeness or distance to God depends on the nature of suffering and pleasure. God often punishes the good in order to make them suffer--in fact God is close at hand at the time--as the father punishes his loving sons for their own good, as the Bible teaches (Proverbs 3:12). God draws near to the humble and contrite in heart (St Augustine 1907, p. 74). The prophets in the moral rectitude have the insight to predict the future unerringly because they are close to God or Truth. Jesus Christ was closest to God (Truth) and even identical with God (Truth). Hence people esteemed him God (Truth)-like or even God (Truth) itself.

Jesus Christ's teachings starting with blessed are the poor in spirit, those who mourn, the meek, those who hunger and thirst for righteousness, the merciful, the pure in heart, the peacemakers, those who are persecuted because of righteousness (Matthew 5:3-10) refer how close people can get to God or Truth. Hence the sufferings make people and nations mature. The Bible repeatedly denigrates the thinking of what to eat and drink, what to wear and what sort of house to live in. It is better to seek suffering and justice than pleasure.

Many Christians believed that the only way they can be really close to God was to cut themselves from the world and live a life of recluse. This is the origin of monastery and the first recorded instance is in Egypt in the third century. It is said that Apostle Saint Mark brought Christianity to Egypt in the early part of the AD first century.

'Love your God' is hard to understand and to put into practice. Hence in Islam this concept is changed to 'Submit to the will of God (Truth)'. Islam means submission and Muslims mean those who submit. The surrender or submission to God may not carry all the meanings of love of God as the Bible intends. The loser surrenders or submits when defeated in war but there is no love on the part of the loser. The Qur'an also sometimes mentions the love of God. For example:

> If you love Allah, follow me: Allah will love you, and grant you protection from your sins. And Allah is Forgiving, Merciful. (Qur'an 3.31)

I expound non-consequential practice of religion in Section 3, Chapter 1 that the ethical conducts may not be superior to human and animal sacrifices, building huge and/or elaborate monuments, giving charity, praying and fasting. Still these conducts can be of value, provided that people carry out these duties in the deep reverence to the divinity (Truth). The focus is not on conducts but on faith. This concept also supports the foregoing argument.

I disclose my conviction in 'Introduction to Series', Book One that Judaism, Christianity and Islam are the same tradition, the latter two originating in Judaism. They came out from the different social and political backdrops but their central theme is the same except for the racism of Judaism. They certainly follow different rituals and customs today indicating different ways of expressing their reverence to the Almighty.

Constantine the Great (312-337) was the first Roman emperor who embraced Christianity. He became an emperor of the Western Empire and a Christian in 312, and eventually became the sole emperor defeating the Eastern Emperor in 324. He summoned and presided over the first ecumenical council of Christian Church in Nicaea in 325. He wanted to outlaw Christian heresies because the unity of the Christian Church was tied to the unity of his empire. Though there had been several councils to resolve theological disputes in the early church before 324, Nicaea council was accorded the first ecumenical council because of its authority and significance. The Nicene Creed, resulting from this council, upheld strictly a Trinitarian belief.

The ecumenical councils have stood on ecumenism to aim to unify the Christian doctrines since their inception. This came out naturally because Christianity was based on the single book of the Bible, and the church with its strict control could not tolerate any dissenting views apart from the political reason above mentioned. At the second ecumenical council in Constantinople in 381, Arius was condemned. At the third ecumenical council in Ephesus in 431, Nestorius was condemned. At the fourth ecumenical council in Chalcedon in 451, monophysitism was outlawed.

Vatican Council I (1869-70) in Rome was the 20th ecumenical councils of the Roman Catholic Church. This was the first ecumenical council since the Council of Trent in 1563. Vatican Council II (1962-65) in Rome was the 21st ecumenical councils of the Roman Catholic Church.

Section 2 Aboriginal People of Australia

I am going to present the manifestation of the core theories of Judaism-Christianity-Islam in this section, mainly to show that the religious doctrines this chapter deals with are not simply metaphysical concepts but have concrete bases illustrated in history.

I used to think before I started learning religion that religion was, in essence, the same as morals: the religious persons were moral persons and vice versa. However, this premise is entirely wrong as I made clear in the last section. In this section I am going to illustrate this view in conjunction with the native inhabitants of Australia, and Christianity of the invading British.

HMS Endeavour, under the captaincy of James Cook, came within sight of Australia on 19th April 1770 and subsequently its crews landed at the place they named Botany Bay. Captain James Cook claimed the east coast of Australia as the British colony. Subsequently the colonisation of the Australian continent took place. In the process the British killed a large number of the native Aboriginals and established the white domination on the huge land mass. There is nothing strange about this piece of history.

A Dutch man Captain Willem Jansz made the recorded sighting of Australia in 1606. Before this discovery there had been numerous rumours of its existence. Marco Polo learned of it in the 13th century from Chinese traders. (Mercer 1996, p. 499)

One question nagged me for many years without any satisfactory answer, concerning the difference of the moral standards between the native Aboriginals and the colonising British. I had been convinced that the native inhabitants of Australia, as the British found, were ethically superior to the colonising people who were mostly convicts, jailors, soldiers, colonists, and the families.

The Aboriginal people have not gone beyond the developmental stage of hunter-gatherers and have not had any system of writing. However, they have developed extensive trading routes across the continent over the millenniums. This fact is surprising because they have a large number of tribal divisions and language groups with the strong enmities among some different tribes reported: 150 Aboriginal languages are still spoken today. They have not known kings and chiefs, and a council of the tribal elders have decided the communal affairs. In spite of all these observations they have practised the ethical teaching of 'Love thy neighbour' far better than the sophisticated invading British people. These facts make us wonder if all the human progress as we talk about may have any substantiative value to us human beings. However, the Aboriginal people did not devise the concept of 'Love your God'. In the biblical sense this was their limitation. They loved their neighbour naturally as Jean Jacques Rousseau wanted to see. They were not taught about the concept as the Britons were at school or church, but the concept came out of their life spontaneously without any inhibition.

At the initial contact of the two peoples, the Aboriginals were at the stage of idealism and the British were at the high level of materialism. My study of history points out that idealism of a civilisation has to give way to materialism sometime during the course of development, as I make clear in Book One *Idealism and Materialism*. This comes about because of the fierce struggles for survival among the changing environments people are to be placed. It seems that the Aboriginal people did not have survival reasons to radically alter their way of life; they were more or less content with their life.

The Australian public widely recognise the notion that the indigenous people of Australia were on higher moral level than the invading whites, and the white Australians who lived in the bush among the native tribes strongly expressed it. I even spoke with a few of these

Australians who had had the opportunity to make the first hand judgement. A few movies I watched over the years also depicted the native people of the bush on ethically high ground.

However, it is also sadly true that the high ethics of the Aboriginals did not come from the firm and tried convictions and hence many of them degenerated into low morality as soon as the colonising British took away their natural environment. The Aboriginals' high morals were those of the infants and came out naturally and without contradictions: they did not know the good nor the evil like Adam and Eve before they ate the prohibited fruits in the Garden of Eden as the Bible narrates.

One of the fundamental testaments of the Bible is that the faithful, individually or nationally, will withstand and repel any attacks however strong the enemy might be. The promise appears in the Old Testament many times and one of the corner stones of Judaism, hence of Christianity and Islam. I would say the unfulfilment of this testament would bring down the biblical tradition from its foundations. The Bible expresses this point in such verses as:

- Can a woman forget her nursing child or show no compassion for the child of her womb? Even she may forget, yet I will not forget you. (Isaiah 49:15)
- Then everyone who calls on the name of the Lord shall be saved; ... (Joel 2:32).

Whereas the proposition of the biblical theologians that the earth did not move had hardly any impact on the value of the Bible for the faithful: the theologians were advocating their belief that the Bible did not contain an error. Further, the dispute was not so much the proposition was important or not but rather a matter of deciding which--the church or the scientists--were in authority regarding life. This interpretation still holds true today in the institutions such as a family, a firm and a nation: the question is not what is correct but who is in authority. The participants to the dispute know well that what they are disputing about is unimportant but the outcome has an important bearing on who would be in charge of the institution.

The said covenant about the infallibility of the faithful depended on the faith of the followers without any other qualifications such as technical expertise and the organisational strength, both of which the British had in abundance. Why then did the invading British conquer so easily the Aboriginals who were on higher moral ground? The questioner mistakenly equated faith with morals and posed this question. The premise of the Testaments primarily rests on faith more than anything else such as morals of the daily life and material knowledge. The Britons were closer to God of the Bible than the Aboriginals in the sphere of faith, though the former were inferior to the latter in terms of ethics.

The assertion that the core biblical teaching is not morals has also been born out with my life experience. When I was attacked personally (aggression or war on a personal dimension), as far as I can remember, I eventually prevailed over the attackers every time I followed the guide of God. I was strong enough to overcome and win over some enemies. My ethical levels were generally high though the morals were virtually non-existent in the matters of sex and taking revenge for the wrongs I had received. On some occasions, the attackers were too powerful for me; however, strangely my adversaries went down with little or no scheme from me. I had to have patience, since if I had attacked back the mighty enemies I would have been beaten back with dire consequences to me. In patient struggle with these adversaries, I relied on what I read in the Bible and often prayed in desperation. These powerful enemies went down from some unknown reasons. I took their downfall as judgement of God. In fact, the Bible says: If any one stirs up strife, it is not from me; whoever stirs up strife with you [the faithful] shall fall because of you (Isaiah 54:15). According to the Bible, God punished the wrong doers not because I was innocent but because they committed sins against God: I did not have anything to do with the punishment meted out on them.

It is hard to ascertain but I now believe that had I depended on morals, probably I would have lost most of the conflicts. The Bible expressly states that it does not approve those who are arrogant and those who are content with small success as well as those who are confined to ethics. On some occasions when I lost sight of the teachings of the Bible, my foes convincingly defeated me and the memories still smart me. It brought home mercilessly that winning the conflict did not come from my attributes but depended on my continual belief in the Omnipotent.

All in all what is written in the Bible concerning the prevalence of the faithful has proven to be true to my satisfaction, in regard to the Aboriginal people of Australia and my experiences.

The thrust of the argument in this series of books proceeds that idealism must give way to materialism for a people to make a progress in history; the people at the advanced stage of materialism predominates over the people at the stage of idealism. The basic drive of this change is survival of the individuals and societies. Thus the British prevailed easily over the Aboriginals. The two propositions presented, that is, that in the Bible and the above historical observation, matched and produced the same results in this case. What to make if the results do not match? We have to analyse each case to see if the two propositions hold or not.
If two do not match then one or two of them must be wrong. The Bible was written by the people who did not expect that the advanced materialism, particularly after the industrial revolution of the modern era, will govern the people's lives.

Chapter 3 Buddhism

Section 1 Buddhist Doctrines and their Development

The foregoing disclosures are my understanding of Christianity. Let's turn our attention to Buddhism which is the main topic of this chapter.

Buddhism aims at the knowledge of reality, and freedom from ignorance and suffering. The Buddhists try to achieve this goal in taking refuge in the Buddha, the Dharma (the Law, Teachings or Truth) and the Sangha (the Buddhist Community). It is a Buddhist tradition rather a Hindu tradition on which Buddhism is based to avoid mere speculation on life and death but seek liberation from suffering.

Unlike Christianity Buddhism has no bible, no pope and no ecumenical councils of the Christian tradition. There are thousands of canons explaining what the Buddhism is all about. There were councils in the early years but they did not try to impose the uniformity of doctrines. Though Buddhism has moral unity, doctrinal diversity characterises Buddhism. Even within one school there are diverse opinions seemingly not caring about the unity. It is hard for us to follow the doctrines for these reasons alone. I cannot tell if these features of Buddhism is good or bad; strength or weakness. All I know is that I have to pick up the threads as they are at present, if I want to learn about Buddhism. Some of the theories concerning the nature of the realities which I explain under the heading of Haecceity of Buddhism are inherently difficult to understand.

I recall a passage from *The Outline of History* (1920) by HG Wells. He presents his summary of the Buddha's teachings, which, I think, shows his good understanding of the alien religion. He then goes onto the following revelation: the Buddha discoursed that it was evil to try to reform a society in any way.

When I read this statement in my youth, the idea puzzled me as to its intent and correctness, as I would expect it does many readers. The questioning notion remained in my mind for many years, asking myself how that could be true and how we could ignore the sufferings of the fellow humans and how the Buddha reached that conclusion. Though I read a fair number of Buddhist canons over the years, I did not find any text which expressly made the above statement. However, I have been convinced that the teaching referred to by Wells is in accordance with Buddhism, possibly of Hinayanism. This is the view I now take, which is the opposite of my past conviction before reading his book and for some time thereafter. The Buddha reached the above conclusion as a universal truth emanating from his world outlook, irrespective of the social system we may happen to be under. I am sure what would hold for the future of mankind did not interest the Buddha. The Mahayanists seek universal salvation, which is not in accord with Mind Only (or Emptiness) of my understanding.

The Buddha did not care about salvation of the other people. The following celebrated episode in *The Majjhima-Nikaya* well illustrates this observation,

> The Buddha at first was not inclined to teach his doctrines of enlightenment, deeming it too profound for persons imbued with lust, hatred and delusion. However, the Buddha was eventually persuaded to preach by a Brahman. (Wayman 1984, p. 13)

Also the Buddha reluctantly admitted females to the Buddhist community and said that because of admission of women, the Law which would have lasted a thousand years, would last only five hundred years (Eliade 1982, p. 78). Ananda, the Buddha's cousin, an attendant and a constant companion, pleaded on behalf of women. *The Lotus Sutra* says that the Buddha's wife and aunt as well as his son attended the assembly held by him (Watson 1993, pp. xvii, 154).

What Wells summarised as the Buddhist teachings presented under the heading of Four Noble Truths to follow are not really the core theories of Buddhism. Is there any cardinal teaching that may correspond to the cardinal Christian doctrine mentioned in the last chapter, among the myriads of the Buddhist theories? I am going to answer this question in this section while explaining the noncore theories.

Until Gautama was 29 years old, he lived an ordinary aristocratic life of his time. He was good-looking and enjoyed hunting and making love. He married a beautiful niece at the age of 19. There was oral tradition of the Vedantic (of Vedanta) epics, which the Brahmins chiefly monopolised. Vedanta became a part of the Vedas, the sacred writings of Hinduism. Gautama became versed in all metaphysics of his day, learning from every wise man he happened to come across. The method of learning was by conversations and not by books. There were hardly any writings at the time in India among the Aryans. The writing system was introduced relatively late among the Aryans--around 5th century BC. The people preferred to use incantations for memorising and teaching rather than written texts.

The indigenous people created the Indus civilisation (c. 2600-2000 BC) which developed around the Indus River, and the Indus scripts, hieroglyphic, have not been deciphered (Whitehouse & Wilkins 1986, p. 16). The Aryans continued to invade and occupy India from 2000-1500 BC. Both Hinduism with its strict caste system and Buddhism are the products of the Aryans. The Buddha (?563-483 BC) lived and taught around the Ganges River. The Buddha's life is described in conjunction with the various canons, particularly in the Pali Tripitaka (the Three Baskets).

The Buddha after attaining enlightenment at the age of 35 taught as long as 45 years and left a large body of discourses, as he acknowledged himself. He discoursed all his teachings orally and did not commit to writing. (Wells 1925, p. 241) The Buddha is often said to be a great physician who can cure the various illnesses of the mind. O Lord my god, the Heavenly Physician of souls, who woundest and healest, who bringest down to hell and bringest back again [*The Imitation of Christ*] (Thomas a Kempis 1980, p. 243). Also the Qur'an is sometimes called a healing because it is a remedy for the spiritual disease. There are thousands of Buddhist canons which can be broadly classed into three divisions, as clearly shown for the Pali canons, of monastic law, the Buddha's discourses and scholastic treatises. The Buddha denied the existence of a supreme being and esteemed the sacrifices useless. He also rejected the caste system Hinduism advocated. Jesus Christ's ministry lasted perhaps for three years and four Gospels contain his teachings, and each of the Gospels is not bulky by any standard and overlaps in many parts. Arnold Toynbee in his book *A Study of History* ([1948]-1961) talks of Mind Only as the highest point the Buddhists reached. He understood Mind Only as meaning that everything is as appears to the mind.

Pythagoras is sometimes suspected to be the same person as the Buddha since both were contemporary persons who lived in the sixth century BC and some of their teachings bear some resemblance. For instance, Pythagoras said, 'Be it thy use to keep these things in check; the belly first, then sleep, desire and anger' (Harbottle 1897, p. 406). From the Christian tradition comes the similar teaching: Prepare yourself like a man to resist the wicked suggestion of the devil; bridle gluttony, and you will easier restrain all carnal inclination (Thomas A Kempis 1982, p. 65). Pythagoras taught the restraints in everyday life and also held the view of reincarnation, and doctrine of immortality and remembrance of former lives (Guthrie 1975, pp. 36, 249). He also believed in the transmigration of the soul, not the random reincarnation, the nature of life depending on the behaviours in the former life. The Buddha himself did not believe in the transmigration of the soul after death; however, his disciples found in this the stuff of fear they could work upon (Wells 1971, p. 335). The claim of the identical person is ridiculous, not so much for the outright denial of the possibility but for the fact that Pythagoras did not teach the concept of Mind Only (or Emptiness) which is the essence of Buddhism.

Is the universe limited in space? Is there any beginning or end to our time? The Buddha did not elaborate these metaphysical questions and directed his disciples to the more pressing problems of everyday life. The Bible shares the same view.

The Vimalakirti Sutra, a Mahayana text, tells that the Buddhist followers do not have to lead a homeless life and the householders can attain the enlightenment (*The Lankavatara Sutra* 1932, p. xxxvii).

The core theory of Buddhism may be Mind Only (or Emptiness). I am sure that the notion of Mind Only (or Emptiness) sounds strange and even absurd at the early encounter to many people at it sounded so in my early encounter. The theory as the next section spells out is contrary to the thought process people are used to since their childhood, mostly determined by their culture. However, they have to suspect that seeing their daily life is full of woes without an end in sight, there may be something wrong in their way of thinking rather than the world around is crooked as they often tend to claim. I have found over the years that the idea of Mind Only (or Emptiness) explains many phenomena in life and to my surprise many people through the course of human history expressed the similar ideas in different ways, which I disclose in the following Section 3. Without this concept Buddhism does not exist in the similar way without the concept I disclosed in Section 1 of the last chapter under the heading of Quiddity of Judaism-Christianity-Islam these strands of religion do not exist. I hope that after going through this chapter many readers will find the proposition is fascinating in its concept and matches with their life experience and some of them may find happiness based on the true state of affairs.

Four Noble Truths and Eight Right Paths, a part of the Four Noble Truths, are widely quoted. Twelve Chains of Dependence is less well known among the general public. I am to briefly expound these theories in the paragraphs to follow.

The starting point of Buddhism or any other serious religion may be said to be fears and sufferings of people. When people suffer so much in life they naturally seek escape. Many people may find consolation in alcohol, gambling, sex, drugs or any other pleasures they can find. However, a small number of people start enquiring if something may be fundamentally wrong in the way they think. These people try to find a new way of thinking in an effort to relieve their mental pains.

The Buddha taught that life is suffering. After grasping the spiritual bliss of such yogic states, the Buddha added that they were impermanent and subject to change. (Eliade 1982, p. 93) Only deep truth, not superficial truth, can console deeply disturbed people and he came up with the following answers.

If everything has self-essence and is not empty, there is neither good nor evil. Only when this phenomenal world is in a state of constant becoming, we can recognise Four Noble Truths is possible.

Four Noble Truths

- There is suffering in life.
- Its origin is thirst and desire.
- There is a way out of suffering, i.e., cessation of suffering.
- The only way is to follow Noble Eight Fold Paths.

Birth is suffering; decay is suffering; illness is suffering; death is suffering; presence of objects we hate is suffering; separation from objects we love is suffering; not to obtain what we desire is suffering. In brief, the five aggregates which spring from grasping are painful. The five aggregates (or skandhas) are form, feelings, perception, volitional factors and consciousness.

The root cause of suffering may be the gap between what one wants to be and what one is; what one wants to have and what one has. There are two approaches to eliminate the suffering: Adjust one of them to make both virtually identical. The non-religious persons, that is, the general public, try to elevate what one is and has: whereas the Buddha taught to downgrade what one wants to be and has.

The Dhammapada reads:

> Weeds are the bane of fields; lust is the bane of mankind. Hence what is given to those lustless yields abundant fruit. Similarly with hatred, delusion and craving. (Narada 1993, p. 272)

Suffering originates in that craving which causes the renewals of becomings, is accompanied by sensual delight, and seeks satisfaction now here, now there; that is to say, craving for pleasures, craving for becoming, craving for not becoming (Koller 1985, p. 137). In conjunction with gratifying senses, the Blessed One said, 'The various sexual acts, gazing, kissing, smelling and embracing women, may give momentary pleasures but are productive of future grief' (*The Lankavatara Sutra* 1932, p. 103).

> What other things shall the fire feed on but your sins? The more you spare yourself now and follow the flesh, the more seriously will you suffer hereafter and the more fuel will you lay up for that fire. [*The Imitation of Christ*] (Thomas A Kempis 1982, p. 87)

HG Wells wrote in the way of summarising the teachings of the Buddha that there are three principal forms of thirst and desire of life and all are evil:

- the desire to gratify the senses, that is, sensuousness
- the desire for immortality
- the desire for prosperity or worldliness

When all three evils are abandoned, people are said to have reached the higher wisdom, that is, nirvana or serenity of soul.

Noble Eight Fold Paths are:

- Right Views including the acknowledgement of Four Noble Truths
- Right Thought
- Right Speech
- Right Conduct
- Right Livelihood
- Right Effort
- Right Mindfulness
- Right Concentration

We can reach the state of nirvana by mastering the Eightfold Paths. Nirvana is the state in which greed, hatred and lust are extinct, and complete liberation from all the sufferings exists. Extinction is the root meaning of Sanskrit word nirvana. The attributes of nirvana may be:

> All sentient beings are then emancipated from the misery of ignorance and folly, their hearts are filled with love and sympathy and free from the clinging to things worthless (Stryk 1982, p. 297).

The Buddha also discovered the formula of Dependent Origination or the Twelvefold Chain of Origination. *The Principle of Sufficient Reason* is the underlying base for the above formula: for everything there must be a ground or reason why it is (Janaway 1994, p. 4). The following twelve states of mind arise in sequence after ignorance and it is said that every state originates depending on the preceding state.

1. Ignorance including the non-acknowledgement of Four Noble Truths
2. motivations
3. perception
4. name-and-form
5. six sense bases
6. sense contact
7. feelings
8. craving
9. indulgence
10. gestation
11. birth
12. old age and death which mean sufferings

The elimination of ignorance leads to the elimination of old age and death, through the undoing of all the foundations of existence, and eventually leads to extinction and nirvana. The wheel of becoming is also Dependent Origination, in other words causal relations; and passion, hatred and stupidity feed themselves in a cycle. Similarly Socrates taught that virtue is knowledge, and according to the above formula all sufferings start with ignorance and its correction leads to liberation and salvation. Our bodily strength grows old, but the mental vigour of good men is beyond the reach of old age [Xenophon] (Harbottle 1897, p. 386). Callimachus, a classical Greek poet and scholar, wrote: Wisdom is a panacea for every ill (p. 387). According to the Upanishads, only way to gain salvation is to have adequate knowledge of spirit. The first lesson is to deny that spirit has attributes. Plato wrote: Ignorance, the root and stem of every evil (p. 322). We also have a popular saying that knowledge is might. We can explain the second noble truth 'Suffering is caused' aforementioned with Dependent Origination, that is, whatever is dependent on something else.

It is interesting to compare the above Dependence Origination with the observation of St Augustine of Hippo:

> For of a froward will, was a lust made; and a lust served, became custom; and custom not resisted, became necessity. By which links, as it were, joined together (whence I called it a chain) a hard bondage held me enthralled. (St Augustine 1907, p. 157)

Two main philosophical implications of Buddhism may be the concept of non-self and impermanence. The former refers to the non-substantiality of self and things (external world). Dependent Origination can underwrite both concepts. (Koller 1985, p. 155) The Madhyamaka School (the Middle School) regarded Dependent Origination as synonymous with Emptiness of self-nature. Nagarjuna, the founder of this school in the first century, argued that Dependent Origination makes sense only if phenomena were devoid of self-essence.

Everything is relative and interdependent and there is no eternal, unchanging or absolute substance in souls or things. Whatever it may be, it contains in itself the seeds of its dissolution. Desire causes suffering, since both people and what people desire are transitory, changing and perishing. It is the impermanence of the object and subject of craving that causes disappointment and sorrow.

A large number of books are available at the book markets, explaining what the above conceptions entail.

The ultimate aim of Buddhism is said to reach the state of nirvana, which may be the Kingdom of God (or Heaven) of Judaic tradition. In both realms, the human sufferings are unknown. It seems that there are different levels of nirvana and the Buddha taught that nirvana acquired through Mind Only (or Emptiness) is the highest. The Buddha did not define nirvana but mentioned only its attributes. Nirvana (transcendental freedom) is deliverance from suffering. It can be called a void because it is void of lust, hatred and ignorance, not because it is nothingness or annihilation. The permanent reality is nirvana. All the combined forces of phenomenal life are illusions. The reality is defined as uncognisable from without, quiescent, undifferentiated in words, unrealisable in concepts, non-plural. (Stcherbatsky 1977, pp. 48, 87) Nirvana may also be said to be the extinction of futile ideas. Nirvana is beyond description in the similar way we cannot describe the Kingdom of God of Judaic tradition: language cannot impart both. We are given the material we work on; we have to work out what they are. The result would be different according to what we are and what our intellect is. Self-liberation through knowledge is an essential theme of Hinduism, Jainism and Buddhism. However, the Buddha insisted that people can experience nirvana by diligently practising the Buddhist truth.

Buddhism has been criticised that its theories are vaguely indefinite, a display of dreamy thoughts about whose meanings the Buddhist teachers themselves are not quite sure (p. 1). Similarly God of Christianity can become nonsense unless guided properly.

> When karma is used in its concrete sense, it is the principle of activity in the world of particulars; it becomes in the physical world the principle of conservation of energy; in the biological realm that of evolution and hereditary, etc.; and in the moral world that of immortality of deeds (Suzuki 1973, p. 181).

Surprisingly the Buddha taught the middle path to his disciples, urging to avoid both extremes in any matter. Though the Buddha himself underwent all sorts of harsh trainings for six years, he realised that asceticism did not produce good results and was not the right way to go. He reached the state of enlightenment sometime after abandoning self-mortification. Since awakening to the ultimate truth he preached the middle way: we should tread the enlightenment paths in moderation, avoiding both ends of the extreme. For example, if we exert too much, we get tired and fall into sin. Hence after a while we should rest. This is the meaning of Right Effort coupled with the middle path, though the effort in anything we do, such as learning and working, is important. We find another example in the teaching of the Buddha in regard to mindfulness: With mindfulness always present, he is neither over relaxed nor overly spirited in mind (Wayman 1984, p. 361). The Buddha taught that nothing is more useful than well-trained mind. Many eminent people through the course of human history expressed the same opinion. This also matches with my experience in the manufacturing industries.

I have found that we should not carry even such good qualities as friendship, kindness and diligence to the excess, and much less so for such not recommended pursuits as drinking, gambling and sex. When the Buddha delivered Noble Eight Fold Paths, he preached his disciples to follow them 'rightly', implying among other things to tread moderately. Buddhism was not originally asceticism as many people today may tend to believe it is.

St Augustine wept uncontrollably and could not find any reason to live when his dearest friend died. However, after a while he came to understand that even the friendship was a sin against God and hence God punished him as a result. He poured out his soul upon the dust, loving one that must die, as if one would never die. He felt that his soul and his friend's soul were one soul in two bodies; his friend was the other half of his soul. He theorised that any attachments (friendship is one of them) other than to God was evil since they were all perishable, which the fact that his friend died manifested. Only the emotion to God is eternal and imperishable. (St Augustine 1907, p. 57)

Aristotle expressed the middle path in the following verse:

> A mid-point is in a sense the highest point.

The Buddha also taught to avoid two extremes of sensual pleasures and self-mortifications. Satisfying the necessities of life is not evil. We should keep our body in good health. The sensual men are slaves of their passions, and pleasure seeking is degrading and vulgar (Stryk 1982, p. 51). We should also avoid ascetic austerity, which people normally associate with the Buddhists.

The philosophers believe in dualism, that is, nihilism and eternalism. Eternalism arises from embracing a doctrine of non-causation; while nihilism arises from believing in the annihilation of causal condition and in the non-existence of a cause. (*The Lankavatara Sutra* 1932, p. 156)

> If beings are non-existent to you, how can there be any distinction between the wise and the ignorant? Nor will there be anything characterising the wise who discipline themselves for the triple emancipation. Things born of causation are non-existent—this is the realm of the wise; a thing imagined has no reality, yet things are imagined by the theorisers. (p. 266)
>
> The ignorant who cherish the notion of being (realism) and non-being (nihilism), by imagining causes and conditions, are unable to understand that all things are causeless and unborn (p. 269).

The Buddha taught that the ignorant and simple-minded are attached to greed, anger and folly. People are also attached to desire which is procreative and is accompanied by joy and greed. He taught that his disciples must leave these attachments. (p. 140) *The Dhammapada* reads: One should give up anger; One should abandon pride; One should overcome all fetters; Ills never befall him who clings not to mind and body and is passionless (Narada 1993, p. 189). The same scripture goes on: Conquer anger by love; Conquer evil by good; Conquer the stingy by giving; Conquer the liar by truth (p. 190). The Bible teaches similarly: Anger and wrath, these also are abominations, yet a sinner holds onto them (Sirach 27:30).

> Therefore, Tathagata (the Buddha), like the sands of the river Ganga, is free from partiality because of his being devoid of likes and dislikes (*The Lankavatara Sutra* 1932, p. 200).
>
> The triple world of existence is no more than thought-construction, which is discriminated by imagination and relative knowledge; but when [within the mind] a turning away from the course of sense objects and the ego-soul takes place, then we have the truth of suchness (p. 232).

'And in his first sermon--the Sutra entitled 'The Foundation of the Kingdom of Righteousness'--the Buddha declares that self-torture is as harmful as self-indulgence to the spiritual mind.' (Sheowring & Thies 1982, p. 124)

Four Noble Truths briefly explained are not the core theory of Buddhism in the similar way the Ten Commandments are not the core theory of Judaism. As I see, the essence of Buddhism lies in the doctrine of Mind Only (or Emptiness). It seems that the Buddha taught the other theories (Four Noble Truths, Noble Eight Fold Paths, Twelve Chains of Dependence and so on) in order that the lay persons can proceed to a higher level of understanding. He taught the advanced students advanced philosophy such as Mind Only, no-ego and Emptiness. (Lopez 1987, p. 46) Ethics for both Judaic and Buddhist faiths may be milk for the infants, and as they grow old they are fed with proper food of higher truth. Social reform, as for ethics, may belong to the truth at the lower level and should be abandoned in pursuit of the higher truth.

The Mind Only (or Emptiness) concept can be incorporated into the Four Noble Truths. Life is suffering because everything is impermanent and illusory. All the sensations are ephemeral and without self. (Kung et al. 1986, p. 297) If we know that everything is an illusion, then we can avoid and eliminate the pleasures and sufferings of life since illusions cause them, and they are all dreams.

It seems that the Buddha was accused of the incompatibility of the two levels of his teachings. The Buddha taught first the existence of self as an accumulator of the actions and experiencer of the effects. He hoped that his followers would turn away from non-virtues which were causes of re-birth in the lower realms. When his followers were thus ready for the advanced teachings, he delivered the sermon of Emptiness and Void of the true state of the world, negating all the previous teachings. (Lopez 1987, p. 46) We can also say that the Buddha taught various doctrines to bring peace and comfort to all sorts of persons, dull as well as intelligent.

The Buddha said, 'I have two forms of teaching the truth: discoursing and self-realisation. I discoursed with the ignorant and disclosed self-realisation to the Yogin' (*The Lankavatara Sutra* 1932, p. 149).

As a preliminary, the initiates of yoga must master the following restraints; not to kill, not to lie, not to steal, sexual abstinence, not to be avaricious (Eliade 1982, p. 62).

Similarly, according to *Oriental Philosophies*, the moral restraints are considered to be the first necessity to begin the yoga practice. The moral restraints thereof are:

- compassionate love to all living creatures
- good speech
- non-stealing
- non-grasping, meaning to eliminate all desire for possessions
- a vow of celibacy

(Koller 1985, pp. 63-4)

The bottom line is that so long as one is steeped in the world of duality and in illusion, the moral law has its usefulness. Once one has risen above duality, above the pairs of opposites, above illusion, law does not need to regulate him. (Stcherbatsky 1977, p. 88) The New Testament states that the Mosaic Law (the moral laws) binds people but once people come under the faith, they are free from the moral laws (Galatians 3:10-14).

Montaigne wrote the following observations in his *Essays*. A true prayer and religious reconciliation of us to God cannot occur in an impure soul subject even then to the domination of Satan. He who calls God to his assistance while he is in the very act of vice acts like a cut-purse who would call justice to his aid, or like those who put forward the name of God as witness to a lie. (Montaigne 1965, p. 235)

Illusion is a condition of complete error in regard to all elements of existence. So long as we do not perceive illusion as illusion, it becomes reality to us. Heaven and hell are the product of imagination. Just as in sleep we dream that we are suffering from the horrors of hell, but on awakening find that there was no hell, even so illusion is like a state of sleep, and in that condition we experience all the suffering; but once we awake to reality, there is no suffering whatsoever. (Stcherbatsky 1977, p. 88)

The dream comparison has parallel to death. When we die, we leave all happiness and suffering behind: it does not make any difference if we had happy or unhappy lives. The life experience has a lot less impact on us, in fact, absolutely zero than the dreams we have. Pinder wrote, 'Man's but a phantom dream' (Harbottle 1897, p. 494). For this I see, that we, all we that live, are but vain shadows, unsubstantial dreams [Sophocles] (p. 494). Man is but breath and shadow, and nothing more [Sophocles] (p. 494). Freud attempted with some success to set up interpretations to our dreams but according to Buddhism we cannot even do that to our life since our life experience is all nonsense.

The Ten Commandments and the Four Noble Truths are conventional truth of lower level. Both love of God and Mind Only (or Emptiness) are the absolute truth of higher level.

The Buddha lived from ?563 to 483 BC and the Buddhist councils were held:

First Council at Rajagrha in 483 BC (after the death of the Buddha)
Second Council at Vaisali in 383 BC
Third Council at Pataliputra in 350 BC and 247 BC
Fourth Council of Kaniska in AD 100
Fifth Council at Lhasa in AD 742
Sixth Council at Rangoon in 1954-6
note 1: Kaniska refers to the reigning king of the time.
note 2: There is a great deal of uncertainty as to the locations, dates, deliberations and even the above ordinal numbers identifying the councils.

The first three councils were called primarily to discuss the problems of disciplinary rules within the Order of Monks rather than theoretical teachings. The matter of discipline was thought to be more important than the religious-philosophical teachings to get rid of the sufferings. On the second and third council, the theoretical difference of Theravada and Mahayana arose. (Koller 1985, pp. 149-50) The first three councils were important in the development of Buddhism; the Third Council is the most significant resulting in splitting of the Elders and the Great Assembly later to develop to Theravada and Mahayana respectively.

The theoretical differences between Theravada and Mahayana do not look critical among the vast number of similar doctrines the two parties put forward, and two schools lived harmoniously most of the times. However, it seems that the rivalry between Theravadins and Mahayanists can be at times quite strong and emotional. The Mahayanists proudly call their sect Mahayana (Greater Vehicle) and contemptuously call Theravada Hinayana (Smaller Vehicle). Theravadins insist that their teachings are the original teachings of the Buddha. One Mahayanist text says that is not the case and primitive Buddhism prevailed before Hinayana Buddhism developed and the Pali texts are biased to some extent, and Mahayana represents the true spirit of the Buddha. (Suzuki 1981, pp. 22-4)

Theravada placed the emphasis on self-discipline; the Buddha taught to reach to the enlightenment with diligence. Whereas Mahayana placed its emphasis on faith. Realism characterises the former, whereas idealism and absolutism the latter. In any case, Buddhism is essentially a way of life, not a philosophy about life. (Koller 1985, p. 151)

The Lankavatara Sutra, a Mahayana text, stresses 'Do not rely on others' and 'Strive yourselves' and at the same time emphasises that unless the power of the Buddha helps the faithful they will never be able to reach to the salvation (*The Lankavatara Sutra* 1932, p. xviii) in the similar way the New Testament emphasises the redemption by Christ for the salvation of the faithful. This sutra as for the other Mahayana Buddhist texts stresses the notion that whatever enlightenment one gains, one must share with one's fellow human beings (p. xvi). Also we find in the sutra the following stanza: The Buddha has penetrated into the minds and thoughts of all beings, moves about everywhere and knows everything (p. 12). This reminds us of omnipresence and omniscience of God in the Christian Bible.

	Theravada	Mahayana
Idealised personage	Bodhisattva and Arhat	Bodhisattva and Buddha
Type of enlightenment	Individual	Universal
Ideal	Nirvana	Buddhahood
Language expressed	Pali	Sanskrit

Some terms may need clarification since a large number of people expressed their opinions as they thought correct.

The Buddha (the awakened one) is a historical personage, variously referred to as:

- Gautama (family name) Siddhartha (personal name); Gautama came from the Kshatriya class and was a noble.
- Sakyamuni (Sage of the Sakya clan)
- Tathagata (He who has Thus Attained or He who has arrived at Suchness)
  note: Tathata means Thusness or Suchness.

A buddha or buddhas are generic title for any enlightened being before and after Sakyamuni. For example, Amitabha was a buddha. A bodhisattva is one who is intent on enlightenment but not as advanced as buddhas; a bodhisattva is a potential buddha (a buddha-to-be). This term appears in both Hinayanism and Mahayanism but particularly emphasised in the latter. The Hinayanists strive to become arhats (perfect ones). Contrary to the above general rule people address the Buddha as arhat in *The Lankavatara Sutra*, a Mahayana text.

The Buddha did not make use of Sanskrit, the sacred language of ancient Indian tradition comparable to Latin in the Western tradition, but he taught in a Middle India language, Pali, that is, the colloquial language of his time. It seems he was born to Magadhi language, a language closely related to Pali. Pali and Magadhi were Prakrit, vernacular languages often contrasted with Sanskrit. (Ostler 2006, p. 178)

In the early Buddhism as for early other Indian religions the teachings were not committed into writings but transmitted orally. Chanting and memorising were the important means of learning the doctrines. For incantatory effect, the language used was formulaic and repetitive, which was retained even after being put into writing. The transmitters wanted to make sure that the teachings were not revealed to unqualified or unworthy persons. (Watson 1993, p. xx)

Immediately after the death of the Buddha in 483 BC, the followers started to compile his teachings into *The Tripitaka*, three part Buddhist canon in Pali language. The first basket is known as Vinaya, dealing with the monastic laws, that is, the rules governing the Sangha.

Ananda, who was the Buddha's servant for 25 years, was the only man who heard and memorised all the Master's discourses. His dictation made up the body of the Sutras (the second basket). The third portion known as the Abhidharmma basket contains the earliest systematic reflections of the dharma dealing with philosophical and psychological issues. The third basket was produced between 300 BC and AD 100, and the authors made every effort to explain the abundant contradictions in the sutras. (Eliade 1982, pp. 210, 217) However, the majority of the canons were transmitted orally until the first century BC.

After a few centuries the sermons were written down, forming the basis of a huge corpus of scriptures called the Sutras. *The Tripitaka* became the canon of Theravada Buddhism.

Mahayana may be said to be the revolt of laymen and laywomen against the ascetic spirit of exclusion pervading among early advocates of Buddhism. We can see the similar revolt by the Protestants against the strict rules of the Catholics in the history of Christianity. Some four hundred years after the death of the Buddha, a large corpus of literature to be known as the Perfect Wisdom Sutra gradually came forward. *Sermon on the Perfect Wisdom* which appeared towards the end of the first century BC may be the earliest documentation of Mahayana. The Hinayanists do not recognise these texts as the words of the Buddha for the most parts.

The contact with the Hellenistic culture opened the new Indian culture. The Greco-Buddhist sculpture of Gandhara is only one example but important since they initiated the anthropomorphic representation of the Buddha. *The Lankavatara Sutra*, a Mahayana text, was not discourses delivered by the Buddha though the text takes that format (*The Lankavatara Sutra* 1932, p. xlii).

Though the biography of the Buddha does not emphasise, most of what he taught came from the ancient Indian religion of Brahmanism and Hinduism, in the same way most of what Jesus Christ taught came from Judaism. The Buddha and Christ went further than the traditional religions and to the limit such that nobody could go any further. The Mahayanists renewed and enriched the Buddhist heritage by incorporating the available (Hinduism is one of them) and new ideas with a liberal and compassionate spirit.

Mahayana emerged as a form of Buddhism by the first century BC, after breaking away at the Third Council from the orthodox Buddhism. The texts of the former acquired the present form between the AD first century and the fifth century.

The term Mahayana was invented at the third or fourth century when the doctrinal struggles reached a climax. Mahayanism does not confine itself to the teaching of the Buddha but incorporates the various teachings of the various buddhas provided they do not contradict the original teachings.

The Hinayanists insisted that their doctrines were what the Buddha originally taught, and he preached only his or her salvation. The Theravadins (the Hinayanists) clearly differentiated the roles of the monks and laymen and did not consider that the laymen could attain enlightenment. In general usage, Hinayana and Theravada mean the same and are used interchangeably; however, some authors make the distinction between the two and Theravada is only one among the various Hinayana doctrines. I follow the general practice in this regard. The Mahayanists addressed the teachings to the believers who left the household as well as who were in the household. The Mahayanists vigorously attacked the view of the individual salvation and advocated the salvation of all sentient beings. The Mahayanists taught that unless we strive at the universal salvation, we cannot reach the level of highest enlightenment, that is, Buddhahood.

Hinayanism strive for individual salvation; Mahayanism for universal salvation. These different outlooks exhibit as different theorisation, for example, on nirvana. The Hinayanists argue that nirvana is the annihilation of the notion of ego-substance and of all the desires arising from this misconception. The Mahayanists agree with the proposition but further argue. To long for nirvana and to shun worldliness are of dualism; we are free from dualism only if we do not long for nirvana and shun worldliness. Those who see only the transitoriness of existence are nihilists, and those who see the eternality of nirvana are eternalists. Both views are incorrect. Thus the Mahayanists should strive for the middle path of nirvana: the intellectual comprehension of truth and the realisation of all embracing love among his fellow creatures. (Suzuki 1973, pp. 359-60)

The doctrine of Void is the foundation of both Hinayana and Mahayana philosophies.

The Buddha instructed the Sangha to be run on democratic principles. The Sangha referred to the Community or the Order of monks and nuns, and in a lesser degree of laymen and laywomen. In the rules of the Sangha or monastic codes for both schools, there are four gravest sins which lead to the expulsion from the monastery: sexual intercourse, theft, murder and exaggeration of one's miraculous powers. There are other rules, transgressions of which carry lesser penalty, such as drinking and lying.

Seeing the success of the Buddha the other religious leaders attempted to subvert the Sangha and to assassinate him (Davison 1993, p. 39).

The Hinayanists basically looked at the Buddha as a human, though the Pali scriptures occasionally credited the Buddha to perform supernatural deeds. *The Saddharmapundarika Sutra,* a Mahayana text, started the concept that the Buddha was not a mere human being but a supernatural being (Suzuki 1930, p. 91). The Tathagata will, by his extraordinary virtue of the sustaining power, cure the mute, the blind and the deaf of their deficiencies (*The Lankavatara Sutra* 1932, p. 89).

During Vietnam War, the Vietnamese Buddhists burned themselves in protest against the war. These monks were the Mahayanists whose aim was universal salvation. The Hinayanists would not have behaved as these monks did, because they were concerned only with individual salvation. The Chinese introduced Mahayana Buddhism to Vietnam during the T'ang dynasty (Ostler 2006, p. 146).

Buddhism did not have a dominant role in India before the Muslims overwhelmed it in the twelfth and thirteenth centuries.

The essence of Buddhism and Christianity do not lie in achievement of happiness of the followers or ethics, though originally people sought the religions to escape from the pains and sufferings. They are the revelation of the life views, which the originators projected as truths. The faithful carry out what they believe in, whether they receive reward or punishment from humans or deity, whether they are happy or not. They follow the truths irrespective of consequences, simply because they are true and right. They can be mocked or even persecuted in so doing. Thus viewed, these religions appeared to be great, untainted by any selfish motives, which is in fact the reason why they have survived the test of time to the present day. After the commercialisation of society, people gave the moral and ethical systems new interpretations such that people felt that right conducts were conducive to the interests of the self and the society.

I am going to disclose my understanding of the Mind Only (or Emptiness) theory in the next section. I made it a policy to explain the theory in conjunction with the familiar occurrences in life rather than to treat the subject as a lofty and cold idea divorced from our life. I also deal the subject in a modern fashion for the general public to be able to understand readily. The Buddha, as for Jesus Christ, adopted these approaches when he preached.

I use the concept to illustrate its use in Book Five *The Sexual Laws*: Section 13, Chapter 1 is particularly relevant.

If you read the specialised books on Mind Only (or Emptiness), you will find they expound the theory in a much more vigorous manner. Although the Bible is easily accessible for the general public the world over, the theory of Mind Only (or Emptiness) is not widely known in the West as well as in the East. I hope that this section may inspire some readers to learn more about the theory.

Section 2 Mind Only (or Emptiness): Haecceity of Buddhism

Haecceity means the discrete properties or characteristics of an entity which determine its individuality. In the absence of more suitable word I had to settle on this philosophical and difficult word.

The highest truth cannot be expressed by language but can be revealed only intuitively to the religious consciousness (Suzuki 1973, p. 105).

All Buddhist schools have the following fundamental propositions whatever different views of minor importance the various schools of Buddhism may propose, and the propositions share the same fate and all stand or fall together:

All is momentary.
All is empty.
All is without self.
All is such as it is.
(p. 140)

Against the above general statement some sects of Buddhism affirm the reality of persons as bearers of the elements and components of personality (Yoshinori 1994, p. 26).

Tathata (Suchness, such as it is; or Thusness) is the essential nature of reality or quiddity of all phenomena. It can mean Emptiness but has more positive overtones. Suchness symbolises concepts of human acceptance and assimilation of any situation. If persons are worried about such phenomena as injustices in the society, starving millions, or wars, they are not looking at the world or life in a way Buddhism teaches. The evils around them do not disturb the Buddhists, and they esteem the world or life such as it is, not passing the judgement of any phenomenon if it is good or bad. Suchness is the mentality free from duality or dualism, in other words, of non-duality or non-dualism, and it is the realm above the good or the bad; pure or non-pure; to be or not to be; it is (eternalism) or it is not (nihilism); moral or immoral; object and subject; justice or injustice; war or peace. (Suzuki 1973, pp. 99-103) Some Buddhists declare non-duality as freeing themselves from words and concepts (Yoshinori 1994, p. 142).

Suchness is the ultimate principle of existence, and the essence of the Buddha, and is known by many different names. The Buddha is a concrete manifestation of suchness (Suzuki 1973, p. 103).

The Buddhists argue that the momentariness or changeability is the essential feature of life and hence the strongest evidence for the non-existence of individual things as realities.

Things are empty and illusory so long as they are particular things and are not thought of in reference to the All that is suchness and reality. Buddhism makes no distinction between being (world) and thought (mind). The world is a manifestation of suchness. Suchness means suchness of existence. We can only state absolute suchness as void or it is not so. (pp. 100-41)

Conditional suchness is a world of particulars; it manifests as various phenomena in nature and various activities such as passions, aspirations, imaginations and intellectual efforts in humans. Absolute transcendental suchness defying all means of characterisation does not have any direct significance in the phenomenal world and human life. Conditional and non-conditional, or, the phenomenal world of causality and the transcendental realm of absolute freedom: they correspond to relative truth and transcendental truth in the field of knowledge.

(pp. 108-10)

There have been two predominant schools in Mahayanism—Madhyamaka (Middle Way) and Yogacara (Mind Only). The former emphasises logical analysis and dialectics and its central theme is Emptiness or Void; the latter, meditation and psychological analysis, and its central theme is Mind Only. The concepts of Emptiness and Mind Only appear in Hinayanism but the above two schools of Mahayanism fully developed them. Emptiness and Mind Only are the ultimate realities, so each school insists.

Nagarjuna and his principal disciple Aryadeva are credited with founding Madhyamaka school in the AD first century. Nagarjuna's most important work, *The Mulamadhyamakakarika,* consists of about 450 verses in 27 chapters dealing with separate topics. Maitreyanatha, Asanga and his brother Vasubandhu developed Yogacara (yoga-practice) school in the 4th century, claiming corrections to the difficulties the earlier Madhyamaka school experienced. Yogacara literature is extensive, and notable among them are *Scripture on the Explication of Underlying Meaning*, *The Lankavatara Sutra, Samdhinirmocana Sutra* and *The Avatamsaka Sutra.* Yogacara school embraced the doctrine of Emptiness but developed it along the line of mind analyses.

Madhyamaka school emphasises that the world or life is empty, that is, it is inherently unreal, conditional and transitory, whereas Yogacara school emphasises the unsubstantiality of impact on mind from the external world even if they admit the external objects, words or concepts may have some substance. Both schools teach that to reach the ultimate truth people have to go through the religious practice, the latter emphasising yoga.

In this book I ignore the different theorisations of the two schools on the belief that both points to the same doctrine that everything is an illusion though presented differently and besides the different approaches do not interest the general public. The presentations of the theories in this chapter are eclectic, not emphasising the source of the school. The differences of the two schools have not interested me in the same way the different approaches to Christianity between Catholicism and Protestantism have not; both hold the same doctrines as expressed in the Bible.

The Mind Only (or Emptiness) theory states that the world has no substance except as appear in our mind. It is all thought-construction, though the theory does not deny the existence of mind. All phenomena, of the world and ultimately of the mind, are devoid of self or substantiality. All that is in the world is devoid of work and action because all things have no reality like an image magically created. (*The Lankavatara Sutra* 1932, p. 20) The world or life is empty in the sense that there is no substantiation for our existence. Emptiness simply means conditionality or transitoriness of all phenomenal existence. The world as it appears to us is an illusion, a void, an emptiness or maya but we erroneously imagine that the phenomena we experience are real and act accordingly. When people fail to see the truth, people have disturbance. People, being attached to the external world, enter into a dualism and there arise all kinds of disaster such as birth, aging, disease, death, sorrow, lamentation, pain, despair, etc. (p. 156) We have cherished, the culture nourishing, the view that the world has some solid quality since our childhood, and hence most of us don't doubt the erroneous outlook, which is the root of all sufferings. The objective world is the manifestation of mind itself and all the sufferings arise from the discrimination of the world. Cessation of the discrimination leads to the cessation of ignorance, desire, deed and causality; hence all sufferings. The Buddhists teach us everything is an illusion or delusion. The outer world of form and name and the inner world of thought and feeling are both no more than the construction of mind. Every object and every being are relative, impermanent, and not worth attachment. Even the qualities of goodness and evil which the elementary Buddhist doctrines, as I explain in Section 1 of this chapter, vigorously uphold are nonsense: they are all in vain and not worth adhering to. The right and the wrong of the moral rectitude are all the creation of the minds and we cannot substantiate both qualities in our life to our ultimate satisfaction. People should leave the moral realms. Even birth and death are not worth thinking about. Mind Only (or Emptiness) manifests in our daily life when we say that we can believe in whatever we like to believe.

The Buddha taught worldly, conventional or expressional truth; and the absolute truth. We can express the former with the language but not the latter that is inexpressible and beyond conventional wisdom. The only way we can get to the latter is through the former. All the doctrines the Buddha taught are compatible with emptiness; emptiness characterises every term in the system of expressional truths. (Robinson 1976, p. 49)

Passions and wrong views arise from mistaking impermanence for permanence, non-self for self, impurity for purity, and suffering for pleasure. These misconceptions enslave worldlings in the domain of desire, form and the formless. Further, we have to go beyond the realm of dualism: existence and nonexistence; religious and worldly. (p. 118)

Things known as defiled or pure are false and perceived by the dim-eye (*The Lankavatara Sutra* 1932, p. 233). There are remarkably similar verses in the Bible:

> I know and am persuaded in the Lord Jesus that nothing is unclean in itself; but it is unclean for anyone who thinks it unclean (Romans 14:14).
>
> To the pure all things are pure, but to the corrupt and unbelieving nothing is pure. Their very minds and consciences are corrupted. (Titus 1:15)

There are two kinds of characteristic signs of self-nature; the attachment to words as having self-nature and the attachments to objects as having self-nature. They arise from false imaginings and not seeing all things as they really and truly are. (*The Lankavatara Sutra* 1932, pp. 87, 97)

> What is seen as multiplicity is the mind saturated with the forms of evil habits; because of mental delusions one clings to forms and appearances regarding them as objective realities (p. 236).

What is the emptiness of subject and object? Eye, ear, nose, tongue, body and mind are the inward (subjective) dharmas and all empty. Forms, sounds, smells, tastes, touch objects and mind objects are the outward (objective) dharmas and all empty. (Conze 1975, p. 144) A dharma here means the individual element that collectively constitutes the empirical world.

Buddhapalita cites the following passage from a Hinayana sutra:

> Form is like a ball of foam.
> Feeling is like a bubble.
> Discrimination is like a mirage.
> Compositional factors are like a banana tree.
> Consciousness is like an illusion.
> So said the Sun-Friend [the Buddha].
>
> (Lopez 1987, p. 83)

The common notion of the general public may say that there is a triple concordance of an ego-soul, sense organs and an objective world. That is to say the general public think that an objective world as an ego-soul or sense organs judge is real. However, the Buddha refuted the above common sense and insisted that the cognition is based on error and wrong judgment. (*The Lankavatara Sutra* 1932, p. 153) The Buddha taught that the above three faculties were independent and cannot be correlated. Hence he reasoned the outside world and sense perceptions as transmitted to the ego-soul are unsubstantial and illusory. According to Schopenhauer, women don't see anything but close to them spatially and in terms of time: they take appearance for reality (Schopenhauer 1962, p. 103). The external world is appearance only and its rise is due to habit-energy. Objectivity discriminated makes the world. When the mind recognises that the world is only the reflection of the mind, the discrimination ceases. (*The Lankavatara Sutra* 1932, p. 271) Montaigne wrote that the senses are incapable of cognising the objects correctly, and our judgements through the appearance of the objects are erroneous (Montaigne 1965, p. 454).

The concept that the world or life is an illusion did not originate in the Buddha but appears in the Vedic tradition of the Vedanta (Kung et al. 1986, p. 193). Also the Bible reads:

> All people are grass,
> their constancy is like the flower
> of the field.
>
> (Isaiah 40:6)

> All nations are as nothing
> before him;
> they are accounted by him as
> less than nothing and emptiness.
>
> (Isaiah 40:17)

> No, they are all a delusion;
> Their works are nothing;
> Their images are empty wind.
>
> (Isaiah 41:29)

Interestingly the Bible, the New Oxford Annotated Edition above cited, uses the terms emptiness and empty, which we normally associate with Buddhism, denoting 'devoid of substance'. The Qur'an says:

> Know that the life of this world is only play, and idle talk, and pageantry, and boasting among you, and rivalry in respect of wealth and children: .... whereas the life of the world is but matter of illusion. (Qur'an 57.20)
>
> Only he who is saved far from the fire and admitted to the Garden will have attained the object (of life); For the life of this world is but goods and chattels of deception (Qur'an 3.185).

The Mind Only concept is the fundamental theory of Buddhism and expanded in the various texts as suchness, emptiness, realm of truth, the various will-made bodies, nirvana (*The Lankavatara Sutra* 1932, pp. 133, 240-1), non-duality, the ultimate limit, essence and non-discrimination.

Any act, once committed, does not disappear like a bubble but leaves a good or bad indelible mark on the individual or the universe depending on the nature of the act, good or bad. In point of fact the mere thought before action leaves the mark in the same way. This mark remains until the karma is exhausted or by the counter karma. If the act is sin repentance can atone the sinner. The law of karma applies only in the moral world and does not extend to the other fields such as economics. In fact the law of karma is the eternal ordinance of the will of Dharmakaya in this world of particulars. (Suzuki 1963, pp. 185-91)

The word nirvana existed prior to the Buddha in the sense of annihilation but he developed it to be enlightenment with affirmation and fulfilment. Nirvana becomes synonymous with suchness or Dharmakaya in the metaphysical sense. (pp. 341-2)

Dharmakaya may be compared in one sense to God of Christianity. Nirvana is humanisation of Dharmakaya. (pp. 46, 51)

The world is no more than thought-construction, and there rages an ocean of views as regards with ego and things. Mind Only looks into the reality as it really is in itself and requires the turning-back (revulsion) of the entire system of mentation to attain its significance. The Buddha lectured his disciples that they have to discipline themselves to realise this concept, not by words only but in its significance. The Buddha can pass only the words and the disciples must realise within themselves. Words are subject to birth and death whereas meanings are not. As meanings are free from existence and non-existence, they are not born and have no substratum. This state is sometimes called transcendental truth or suchness of existence. (*The Lankavatara Sutra* 1932, pp. 167, 230)

The Mind Only concept does not deny the existence of the objective world but it esteems that it is all like a dream, a mirage and a magical creation without any substance. The objective world is based on false imagination and Mind Only is the ultimate intuitive knowledge. The individual objects are not solid (realities); they rise because of imagination. As the imagination itself is empty, what is imagined is empty. (pp. 227, 237)

Many Buddhist scriptures use the term Emptiness but it is hard for us to understand it initially. When we see a good-looking box, we think there is something good in it; however, upon opening we find it is empty with some disappointment. Similarly when we imagine whatever we want such as wealth, fame, honour and women, the desire arises in us; however, upon acquiring them, we find nothing in them: We do not get the level of satisfaction we anticipated. This may be another way to explain Emptiness.

All phenomena are empty, that being the true identity. Everything is like empty space, without innate nature, beyond the reach of all words. It is unborn; it does not emerge. It exists only through causes and conditions. (Watson 1993, p. 198)

The Buddhists regard the phenomena (objects)--the individual persons and the world--dependent arising and empty. Whatever exists must both be relatively existent and lack inherent existence. (Hopkins 1983, p. 659) They could not substantiate the objective world of people and material, much less the subjective world of dreams and fantasies. The universe is impermanent or lacking in permanent substratum, and change and sufferings of people characterise it. The Buddha taught that even God, as people popularly believed in India at that time to be the creator and ruler of the world, was an illusion (Kung et al. 1986, p. 293). Mind Only declares that not only things (normally called objects) are empty but people (normally called subjects) are empty.

> The concept of the individual ego is a popular delusion; the objects with which people identify themselves--fortune, social position, family, body and even mind--are not their true selves (*Encyclopaedia Britannica*, 15th edn, sv, Buddhism.).
>
> The cycle of existence (birth, death and rebirth) is marked by impermanence, unsatisfactoriness and lack of a permanent self. It is impermanent because all things, whether physical objects, psychological status or philosophical ideas, undergo changes; they are brought into existence by preceding conditions at a particular point in time, and they eventually will become extinct. It is unsatisfactory in the sense that not only do sentient beings experience physical pains, they also face continual disappointment when the people and things they wish to maintain invariably change. The third characteristic of sentient existence is lack of permanent self. (Lopez 1996, p. 14)

The Dhammapada reads:

> Impermanence, sorrow and no-soul are the characteristics of all things conditioned by causes. By contemplating these one realises nirvana. (Narada 1993, p. 224)

Confucius, standing by a stream uttered the following poem:

> It passes on just like this, not ceasing day and night.

It refers to everything--life, nature, and human problem, and the poem means that everything is in a state of constant flux and impermanence (Chen 1987, p. 22).

Life is a dream. What we experience in our daily life remains in our memory or at least somewhere in our brain, but I have found that it is no different from dreams in our sleep as long as I direct my mind to be so. If people believe that life is only a dream, their attitudes towards life would be entirely different. Moschus, a classical Greek, wrote, 'We that are great and strong and wise, when death has laid us senseless in the hollow tomb, shall sleep an endless sleep that knows no waking' (Harbottle 1897, p. 322).

Psychologically fantasy or daydream is different from realities in that the former escaping from the harsh realities does not contribute to the mental growth of our brains and possibly does not carry punishment even if its contents are sinful. Realities build our conscious selves and have good and bad consequences in the future. We have to make distinctions between dreams and realities for our everyday intercourse with other people. The effects on our brain from these two sets of brain activities are different: the former nurtures imagination though important in some fields of human activities; the latter forms common sense and mental age. For this aspect, refer to Section 7 Cure of Nervous Problems, Chapter 1, Book Four.

No sense of time, place, and conditions appears during sleep. St Paul related death to sleep. (Hall 1984, p. 37)

While we are dreaming in sleep, the dreams are realities for us but upon waking up we cannot substantiate the dreams. In the same way if we imagine what happens after our death, all realities of life are all dreams and unsubstantial.

When children read comics or fairy tales, they normally do not ask if the stories happened in the real world or not: for them the distinctions of the realities and the fantasies are not important. The Mind Only (or Emptiness) concept makes a similar claim that there is no substantive difference between the real and the imaginary.

The comic strips, if done cleverly, can be a source of entertainment and can give good insight into the human nature as well as some ideas in solving the real life problems. The advantage of the comic writers is that the realities do not inhibit or restrain them.

Even the literature which purports to be the reflection of the real life or world is after all approximations of the realities through the eyes and words of the writers. Consequently we can say the literature is only dreams and fantasies of the writers who do not know that fact.

> The sense organs are to be known as Maya, the sense-fields resemble a dream; actor, act and acting--they do not at all [in reality] exist (*The Lankavatara Sutra* 1932, p. 235).

According to worldly knowledge, everything exists: but in ultimate truth none exists; in ultimate truth, indeed, one sees that all things are devoid of self-substance. Although there is no self-substance, there arises something which one perceives [as objective reality]--this is called worldly knowledge. (p. 235)

Truths, the Buddha and every other teaching are in fact products of imagination (p. 236).

There are five sense organs in our body: eyes, ears, nose, tongue and body. The sensations result from the recognition of the external world by these organs. Most sensations of sight, hearing, smell, taste and touch create good or bad impressions in our mind, thus leaving like or dislike feelings. By our habit since our birth, we are conditioned to choose good sensation and avoid bad sensation. The problem is that this attitude is not in accord with the true state of the real world. These perceptions are nothing but a reflection of illusory external world through illusory sense organs. The adherents are only temporarily satisfied and ever seek more good perceptions which are ultimately false. This state of affairs eventually leads us to unhappiness. Thus Buddhism teaches us not to attach to what we see, hear, smell, taste and touch. Consequently according to Buddhism we should not appreciate any paintings, sculptures, music, perfumes, or any man-made objects such as buildings and bridges: all of these objects are designed to please our visual aesthesia, apart from the functional requirements if any.

The Bible clearly states this point when one commandment strictly prohibits makings of any images of humans or animals and also it makes frequent references to make light of the material existence. However, it approves listening to music. Music may be an exception to the above rule. There is not a command which states that we should refrain from listening to music anywhere in the Bible. In fact many Psalms have notes that we should read them in accompaniment with music: music orients people to be receptive to the idea Psalms contains. Buddhism and Islam do not recognise that even music is necessary to humans.

Refraining from the sense enjoyments is a necessary but not sufficient condition to reach nirvana which involves loftier concepts. Thus the Buddha directed not to be attached to anything existent—property, family and friends—and to walk all alone. He taught not to keep property such as money, grain, land, slaves and cattle.

Unreliability of sense perception thus preached made its way to Greece. Pyrrho of Elis (c. 365-275 BC) taught people to suspend all judgements since the senses are unreliable. (Cotterell 1993, p. xii) He held the view of extreme asceticism.

Everyone thinks and behaves on the belief that they are on the right, which is probably the seeds of most conflicts and wars. Mind Only (or Emptiness) explains why there are so many differing views and opinions for practically every subject in this world. Some are merely different approaches to achieve the same end. Some are diametrically opposed in regard to the aims and the means. Some do not recognise the existence of the other view: for example, the communists do not believe that religion is necessary to humankind. The ethics does not explain what happens in the society, seeing that we have a lot of thefts, cheatings, lies and murders. The moral people would not comprehend why people go against the morals. Mind Only (or Emptiness) does not have any problems in incorporating the various unethical conducts of people into our thinking process. Mind Only (or Emptiness) says that what people believe in are reflection of their mind and consequently their beliefs are all illusions. Thus, Buddhism indoctrinates that their beliefs are not worth clinging to and tries to remove the source of conflicts.

The Buddha emphasised that all his teachings should correspond to our daily life rather than metaphysical exercises which are beyond our daily experience. The Buddhists naturally try to conform to the concept of Mind Only (or Emptiness) in their life, not just being satisfied with the conceptual understanding.

Hinduism also teaches that the mind and the world are inseparable and one needs only look within oneself to discover the truth (Stryk 1982, p. 306). Thus yogis try to become one with the Supreme Being through concentration. Hinduism regards man's universe to be an illusion. (Toynbee et al. 1968, p. 71)

We need food, clothes and shelter: these are necessities of life. We have to have them with a right attitude such that we don't indulge in the enjoyments of the senses or vain glory. We eat and drink to get nourishment, not for pleasure stimulating olfactory and palatal discrimination. We clothes ourselves to keep warm and for social courtesy, not for showing off. We live in a house to protect ourselves from the elements and robbers, not using it as a symbol of wealth. These necessities of life should be taken only so far as necessary and should not become a source of enjoyment in any way. We should not drink intoxicating liquids, should not gamble and should not have sex. Further, Buddhism does not recognise the need for such items as music, perfume, sculpture and painting since all what they do is to stimulate our mind through the sense organs: music for the ears, perfume for the nose, sculpture and painting for the eyes.

The Bible, rather surprisingly, takes a similar position. The Old Testament repeatedly states that we should not make graven images nor draw any likeness of anything on earth. The ultimate object of prohibition is idolatry: making idols of God and serve them. The Bible does not state why the above ordinances must be upheld: it takes the form of revelation from God as for all the other precepts in the Scripture.

Mind Only (or Emptiness) does not confine itself to the realm of senses, and extends its prohibition to such human longings as fame, power, wealth and sex. It disciplines that these human pursuits are also products of our mind and hence all illusions. Thus Buddhism tells us not to pursue fame, power, wealth and sex since they are like mirages and give us only temporal happiness with a lot of anxieties and occasional miseries. We should train ourselves so that we are beyond flattery and unfair criticism. The teaching makes a point that we do not store up the material possessions such as money, assets, and even food and clothes. Many people who were fortunate enough to accumulate a large amount of these worldly possessions testified, through millenniums, that the ownership did not contribute to their happiness in the long course of their lives, though certainly they gave temporary happiness. These material objects can be compared to the toys of a toddler: If he is given a good toy, he is happy but soon loses interest in it; if he is taken away of it, he cries but soon forgets about it.

The author of Ecclesiastes, possibly King Solomon, uttered the following famous verses (Ecclesiastes 1:2), after having all the enjoyments of the world: Vanity of vanities, says the Teacher, vanity of vanities! All is vanity. The word 'vanity' can be replaced by such terms as illusion, emptiness, voidness, vacuity or meaninglessness without losing the essential sense of the verses. Many of the ideas in Ecclesiastes are unique in the biblical traditions. The author, for instance, seriously questions the value of human existence and laments the injustice of the society, not referring to the faith in God. The messages of Ecclesiastes are philosophical, not religious. The ideas in Ecclesiastes come close to Buddhists' assessment of life, though some biblical scholars find Ecclesiastes so totally out of characters of the biblical tradition that they should leave it out of the Bible altogether. Some scholars inferred that the author wrote the Book of Ecclesiastes based on Greek philosophy. (Eliade 1982, p. 260)

As a matter of fact the cardinal teaching of 'Love of God' in the Bible may be based on the observation that life and the world are all illusions.

There are some differences between Ecclesiastes and the concept of Mind Only (or Emptiness). Let's cite an example. Anyone who is among the living has hope!—even a live dog is better off than a dead lion! (Ecclesiastes 9:4) However, Mind Only (or Emptiness) does not make a distinction between the living and the dead; a dog and a lion, and uniformly asserts that they are all illusions. Also Buddhism does not lament the injustice in the society.

Only the Buddhist scripture *The Lankavatara Sutra* uses the term 'no-birth' or 'unborn' often for the Buddhist term Emptiness but they all denote the same concept and are interchangeable. No-birth in its root means everything is not born, not in the physical sense but in the sense that it has no self-nature. The ignorant discriminate the external world as realities: As a matter of fact the external world is non-realities and is expressed only by the words of people. Things are devoid of self-substance, not final, irreducible realities, for they have never been created (born) and they are what they are from the beginningless past. (Suzuki 1930, p. 98) No-birth also denotes abandonment of all the philosophical views (*The*

Lankavatara Sutra 1932, p. 174). A Mahayana master wrote *The Lankavatara Sutra,* which is said to include all the important teachings accepted by the followers of Mahayanism at the time (p. xi). The external world is only the reflection of mind and has never been born, but owing to the discrimination and false intellection practised since beginningless time, that is, by habit-energy or memory, people perceive that the material objects, that is, body, property and abode, have reality (p. 38). Reality as it is or mind in itself is also called suchness or the sameness of things. They unify all forms of antithesis which constitute our actual world of sense and logic, and transcend all our reasoning and discriminations. (Suzuki 1930, p. 99) Multiplicity of objects evolves from the conjunction of habit-energy and discrimination; it is born of mind, but people regard it as existing outwardly (*The Lankavatara Sutra* 1932, p. 133).

Bodhidharma, father of Ch'an School Buddhism, made use of *The Lankavatara Sutra* effectively.

The foregoing observations are equivalent to the statement 'Everything is an illusion', which is what the Mind Only (or Emptiness) proposes to be the cardinal state of life or the world.

If we ask the people in the temporal world why then they want to become rich, famous or powerful, they are probably at a loss for a reasonable explanation. The inner urges some people feel towards these desired goals are akin to the sexual urge and they feel they have to acquire the desired ends irrespective of the means and consequences.

A strange aspect of Buddhism, and Christianity for that matter, is that these teachings recognise morals or virtues, and excellence of mind. If the Buddhists believe that everything is an illusion, why do they see any values in ethics and excellence of mind? Further, what is the sense in trying to understand the concept of Mind Only (or Emptiness) if everything is a reflection of mind? The author of Ecclesiastes did not know the answer and wrote (Ecclesiastes 2:16): For there is no enduring remembrance of the wise or of fools, seeing that in the days to come all will have been long forgotten; How can the wise die just like fools? He still thought that to be wise was better than to be foolish and lived his life accordingly.

Faced with the objection that if all is void, then the Four Noble Truths, the Order of Monks and the Buddha himself must be worthless, Nagarjuna answered by the following remarks in *The Madhyamika-sastra* (*Discourse in the Middle Path*): The Buddha speaks of two truths, one in the absolute sense, the other conventional and relative. One who does not see the distinction cannot hope to understand Buddhism. (Stryk 1982, p. 283)

> Relative knowledge takes place where there is something resembling the external world; transcendental knowledge belongs to the realm of suchness (*The Lankavatara Sutra* 1932, p. 238).

Probably the two truths mentioned above are not two independent teachings as the above argument might infer. Unless people are firm on the conventional truth, that is, they are articulate morally and in the conventional wisdom, people, with a negligible percentage of exceptions, are not conducive to the absolute truth.

The following episode highlights the concept of Mind Only (or Emptiness) in a real life situation: WG Burchett, a practising communist, in his book bitterly criticised the European in his behaviour of the event which took placc in China during the war.

The wall separated the Europeans in a relative comfort and the starving Chinese. The author focused his attention to the fact that a European was desperately looking for his lost dog, ignoring the fact that many Chinese were suffering and even dying on the other side of the wall. Mind Only (or Emptiness) does not differentiate between a dog and a human being and between suffering and ease. The theory sees things as they are and does not wish to have its own standard imposed on people except that all things are really only the reflection of mind. It did not enter to the head of Burchett that there were other perspectives in life than his own, which caused a lot of distress in him as a result: He assumed that people were more important than dogs and comfort was preferable to suffering. If he had known the proposition of Mind Only (or Emptiness), he would have kept his peace about the above incident: He would have theorised that his view was not necessarily correct and in fact what he witnessed was an illusion. The Mind Only (or Emptiness) theory does not regard one concept is better than the other. For example, it does not rate politics or economics as better human pursuits than sport or music, nor compassion towards humans is preferable to the compassion towards dogs. Mind Only (or Emptiness) regards uniformly everything as the reflection of mind and does not judge one thing, whatever it may be, is good or bad.

Mind Only (or Emptiness) has Social Problem

People most likely shun a person who leads a life according to the theory of Mind Only (or Emptiness), and the person cannot lead a social life. Similarly the spiritual world the Bible creates is so different from the temporal world that if the believer is to follow the life literally according to its teachings, that person has a serious problem in his relation to the other human beings. The followers of both teachings have to alter their behaviours considerably if they want to remain in harmony with the people around. Plato says that whoever escapes with clean breeches from handling the affairs of the world, escapes by a miracle (Montaigne 1965, p. 759).

The Dhammapada says:

> If, as the disciple fares along, he meets no companion who is better or equal, let him firmly pursue his solitary career. There is no fellowship with the foolish. (Narada 1993, p. 62)

The Imitation of Christ says:

> Rare indeed is a faithful friend, who stands by his friend in all trouble. And you, Lord, are the most faithful of all friends, and there is none like you. (Thomas A Kempis 1952, p. 151)

A hermit can master the Mind Only (or Emptiness) viewpoint and live a happy life because he does not have to relate to anybody. The problems arise when a true Buddhist comes into contact with people. People would think the master of Mind Only (or Emptiness) is mad and should be in a mental hospital. The master does not differentiate between the good and the evil. In fact he does not have the judgement criteria of any sort. His way of thinking may be that of a toddler. A toddler may burn down a house playing with matches and it may shoot a person dead toying with a rifle, yet it does not think it has done anything wrong. The toddler does not differentiate the good from the evil in the way the ordinary adults would do.

A hermit does not have to follow the precept 'Love thy neighbour' simply because he lives alone. However, he can still spend time mastering the Buddhist concept of Mind Only (or Emptiness) and the Christian doctrine of love of God. This observation places the latter two concepts higher than the former concept. This matches with the earlier proposition that the latter thinking is absolute and the former relative.

The Buddhists who hold fast the concept of Mind Only (or Emptiness) have to learn to modify their way of thinking to suit the social life if they want to live among people. I would say that people crucified Jesus Christ because he embodied in himself a God-like nature, not accommodating for social life. The Buddha lived among his disciples after enlightenment and had little contact with lay people who might have attacked him for his teachings.

The sages the world over are on the extreme end of the good heart. The criminals are on the other extreme end. The general public shun both types of people, and naturally want to see only their kinds around, that is, people who are neither too good nor too bad in the goodness scale. There is also a definite rule that the good people seek and support the good and just, and on the way try to destroy the evil in the society. The bad do exactly the opposite; they seek and support the evil and injustice, and on the way try to destroy the good in the society.

Buddhism and Christianity in their pure forms do not recognise arts; hence people are apt to misunderstand the true believers. The believers in their enthusiasm do not follow recognised arts in their life. In the life of the ordinary people, the run of the mill appreciations of the various arts--paintings, calligraphy, sculpture and mannerism--are integral parts of their life.

Mind Only (or Emptiness) is against Social Reforms

The Buddha educated his disciples that it was evil to reform the society in any way. This opinion is obvious from the concept of Mind Only (or Emptiness). There is no point in improving the world, since the reformed society is also illusory in the same token as the society before the betterment was illusory. This idea is not the common opinion that we don't agree how we should reform the society nor we cannot achieve what we agree. The proposal against the social betterment is projected as the eternal and irrefutable truth.

I have found that this doctrine is parallel to Judaism, Christianity and Islam with some twist, though the Judaeo-Christian-Islamic scholars, I am sure, would not accept this view as valid. According to the Bible, God punishes people for disobeying God's ordinances. People commit sins and God punishes them as a result. Only way to remedy the situation is for the people to repent and correct their original mistakes. For example, the starving people of the world came about as a result of rebellion against God. If some people with charitable intent try to remedy the sorry state, they are interfering with the judgement of God. I now firmly believe that they should leave the people alone, whatever state--good or bad--they are in. We also find the following verses in the Qur'an:

> Do you desire to guide him whom Allah leaves in error? And whomsoever Allah leaves in error thou canst not find a way for him. (Qur'an 4.88)

The author of Ecclesiastes makes the following resigning comment (Ecclesiastes 1:15): What is crooked cannot be made straight, and what is lacking cannot be counted. This verse probably refers to daily experience of people rather than a large issue of social reform; however, it illustrates the common attitude by the various authors of the Bible that the obedience to God should be the primary concern of the faithful and they should not tackle the social evils. The prophets urge people to return to the call of God and the grace of God will look after them subsequently.

Watching millions of people starving to death will not perturb people imbued with Mind Only (or Emptiness). Wars being waged even in their midst will not trouble them, much less in the distant countries. They will be unmoved if people persecute, slaughter and exterminate them as a race. True Buddhists among the Jewish persecutions by the Nazis would not have had any sympathy to the fellow human beings. They would not have lifted a finger to try to save a life, whether they were somebodies else's or theirs. The Bible well expresses these lines of thoughts, particularly in the Book of Psalms. An example: Therefore we will not fear, though the earth gives way and the mountains fall into the heart of the sea (Psalms 46:2).

Asoka (?273-232 BC), last major emperor of the Mauryan empire in India, establishing Buddhism as the state religion, misunderstood the essence of Buddhism as benevolent charity, in the similar way some Christians misunderstand the essence of Christianity as charity today.

The above scenario reminds me of *The Time Machine* (1895) by HG Wells, though in the fictional story set in the future he deals the point concerned in a disapproving light, and he does not mention the good aspects. This science fiction tells how the monsters bred the future humans to become food for them. The humans are unconcerned with their fate and do not care if the fellow humans get injured or die.

Let's introduce another perspective. We all suffer and die. Hence it is not important for us how we suffer and die. Certainly we go through life; happy times alternating with unhappy times in small everyday cycles as well as in larger eventful cycles. Nobody can remain happy for a long time; in a similar way nobody can remain unhappy for a long time. This viewpoint reinforces the theory that it is evil to try to reform the society. I believe even the great originators of the religions suffered and died, probably not in the same way as the majority of people did: the sages may not have worried for themselves but certainly did for the salvation of mankind.

It is often said that life is like a dream. Then it does not matter at all if we have a good or bad dream. I, on more than one occasion, tried to change the course of the dream for the better, knowing I was dreaming while I was having a dream. The social reformer may be compared to me trying to change the content of a dream. From this perspective also, it is obvious that there is no gains in trying to better our political, economic and social environments in any way.

The teaching of the Third Prophecy also reinforces the folly of various social reforms. After the introduction of the prophecy at the social level, the social reforms make some sense. For more information, please read Book Four *The Third Prophecy* in this series of books. People versed in this book should know well that it is a sheer stupidity to try to correct evils of any form and shape, because we cannot expect the population at large before acquainting with this new prophecy to behave in unselfish manner to allow the reforms.

The social reformers and active environmentalists should learn the essence of Christianity or the Mind Only (or Emptiness) or the Third Prophecy. If they master one of the teachings, they will most likely stop any effort to improving their surroundings disgusted with themselves that how silly they are in sparing their thoughts on the social agenda; and will turn their attention to something more useful or beneficial for themselves. These people, once they are enlightened, may agree with Theodorus of Cyrene, a classical Greek, who said: It is unjust for a wise man to risk his life for the good of his country, and endanger wisdom for the sake of fools (Montaigne 1965, p. 221).

<u>According to Mind Only (or Emptiness) Life or World has no Inherent Values.</u>

We find love if we think life is full of love; we find hate if we think life is full of hate. Life is, in this sense, neutral. It is up to an individual to discover what life is really made of.

My experiences and observations support the assertion of the last paragraph well. People who equate life or world to love are right; people who equate it to hate are also right. We cannot alter the fact that some people lived and died believing in one of the two views carried to the extreme. It does not make any sense to say that the other view was right since they knew and practised only one view in the course of their life. The only correct conclusion we can draw from these assessments is that life or world has no inherent worth; each individual chooses what each takes out from life. When both views which seem right on their own but seem to contradict with each other like the argument under consideration, the only way to resolve the situation seems to assume the subject has no substance except as appears to our mind.

When we observe an object under a microscope we can obtain many colours as we change the settings, and we can say that a colour under the microscope is an illusion.

Jesus Christ believed in and practised love; the Jews around him believed in hate. The Jews could not accommodate the possibility that life was love and sought to destroy the man who said they were wrong. According to the Mind Only (or Emptiness) concept both views were in fact correct in their own ways and at the same time both views were wrong in that both did not accommodate the other. Average or ordinary people love or hate according to the circumstances and live in the mixture of love and hate. Montaigne wrote that life is neither good nor evil in itself; it is the scene of good and evil according as you give them room (Montaigne 1965, p. 65).

In the first book of this series, I present idealism and materialism as if both were correct. In fact the two ideologies are mutually exclusive in their purest forms and the history of the world has shown that the firm believers of one doctrine fiercely attacked the other. It is wrong, in any case nothing will change, to judge that one of the ideologies was on the right track or in the wrong. Life or the world does not have any inherent values except for people who make out to be in a certain way. I say that all the doctrines are right and at the same time they are all wrong though this statement sounds self-contradicting: they have no substance except as appears to the minds of the believers. This thinking is the idea of Mind Only (or Emptiness).

Growing Old and Mind Only (or Emptiness)

The children will find the concept of Mind Only (or Emptiness) hard to accept, rather I would say that the doctrine will bewilder them and they cannot see any sense behind it. The incomprehensibility on the part of the children is not confined to the philosophical idea of Mind Only (or Emptiness) and goes to the various subjects. For example, as a child, the media and people around me, that is, the so-called overt culture took the existence of families, various establishments and nations for granted, and their creations and endeavours seemed quite natural to me. I simply did not comprehend why some people wanted to damage or destroy human life or the human creations, as I would suspect most children do not.

Through studying history at high school, a peculiar notion as to the fundamental reasons for a historical event to take place obsessed me at some stage. The word 'peculiar' was used to let readers know that the kind of the question was not raised in a history class as well as I was out of ordinary pupil for good or bad depending on how people assessed me, though I took the study quite seriously. I did not understand why a certain event in history had taken place so recklessly and so randomly: a nation started war with another; some people spent enormous effort and time to accomplish something; an assassin sacrificed his life to satisfy his ego. I wanted to know why people had acted in the way they had and not otherwise. In response to my worry that I did not understand history, my classmate laughed it off, telling me that history has the human endeavours in random and no principles of that description.

After agonising myself thus for about six months during which period I eagerly sought the answer worrying quite a lot, at last I realised the answer to my burning quest. There were no compulsive reasons why the historical events took place in a certain way. History should take place recklessly and randomly because all humans are mortal and they don't have to have deep and convincing reasons for any of their actions. Whatever actions, good or bad, people may choose, they cannot escape one fate they have to face eventually. People responsible for the events must die and people who hear about the events must die also, hence the events, whatever they may be, cannot be important. The above line of thoughts came to me as an enlightenment and I ceased to be worried about the subject. I did not know anything about Buddhism at the time; however, I have come to believe that the solution was one manifestation of the Mind Only (or Emptiness) doctrine.

We can find the similar question and answer in the smoking habit of some people. People eventually have to die if they smoke or not, though the smokers must be aware that the habit may quicken the process considerably for many of them. For many children this line of thought is hard to comprehend.

As people get old, they tend to accept the society and themselves as they are, abandoning the notion what the society and themselves ought to be. Generally this facet shows up that the aged tend to be conservative. The young people, on the other hand, have fresh impressions on new happenings, and people's behaviours out of step from the overt culture are apt to amaze them.

As people get older and hence have more life experience, their way of thinking normally gets closer to the concept of Mind Only (or Emptiness). The aged tend to esteem the curious conducts of some people not so surprising in the light of the foregoing argument; while they were younger, the same conducts simply puzzled and amazed them not knowing what to make of them. There is the other side of this coin. What they learn impress the young people and hence their learning is fast, whereas not many things impress the old people hence their learning progress is slow. The old people are accustomed to think they are dreaming their life and it takes a great deal to surprise them. It was through philosophy, he said, that he had come to be surprised at nothing [Pythagoras] (Harbottle 1897, p. 420).

The following assessment of life that conforms to Mind Only (or Emptiness) would not startle the aged: Human lives, human establishments and nations have no inherent values. Destruction of these human creations is no different from making them. Whatever forms these products of imagination and intelligence may take, they are neither good nor evil. Making and destroying these creations are one and the same action, and everything--creating, destroying, the creations, the creators, the destroyers and the observers--is an illusion.

One way of visualising the essence of Mind Only (or Emptiness) may be to think life in relation to death. Once we are dead, we don't know anything. What we did or believed in while alive counts for nothing when we die. Once we are dead, we know neither love nor hate and the emotion we carried in our life is a void. Death is null and void, which is hard to imagine for us. We try to think death to be the same as sleep because we imagine that to be dead is like to be asleep. In sleep we dream and are promised to wake up. But in death we sleep forever without dreams. Whether we are rich or poor; whether we lived a good life or not; whether we are righteous or unrighteous: all these don't mean anything after death. The Mind Only (or Emptiness) concept teaches us that our beliefs and deeds and even our attributes don't mean anything even while we are alive. Probably the above lines of thoughts may get closest to visualising the Mind Only (or Emptiness) proposition.

Time and Space References

Buddhism does not often refer to space consideration but concentrates on time consideration in explaining Min Only (or Emptiness). I expound the theory in the following paragraphs along with the time consideration together with the space consideration, both of which the general public widely use as effective reasons to explaining the futility of life.

In reference to time, what we experience through our life would be immaterial, though we are in a habit of making it something in our thinking and in our custom. The moment we die, whatever we were and whatever we did in our life reduce to a void. We can conclude with a certainty that everything we go through in our life is less than a mirage upon our death. Just imagine two gigantic dinosaurs in the Mesozoic era were fighting to death. For them, the combat was real and meant a difference of life and death. For us, the result of the struggle is nonsense because of the different time scale. In the same way, our daily struggle of life and even our existence do not mean a thing for people of the future generations.

However a woman may be beautiful she is no longer attractive when she gets old, which comes swiftly for every woman. Hence Buddhism uses this fact to conclude that female beauty is an illusion apart from the belief that it does not recognise anything is inherently beautiful or ugly.

Every individual feels that they are the centre of the universe. People think and act accordingly. They expect that the whole world should serve them and if it doesn't they often get angry or despair. In fact the theory of Mind Only (or Emptiness) teaches people that the premise that individuals feel that they are the centre of the universe is wrong. The earth is only a tiny speck in the universe and people are nothing at all, not even dusts, in the vastness of the universe which does not care in the slightest even if all the humans on the globe disappear. The scientists speculate that the sun was born possibly five billion years ago and has a life of perhaps another five billion years. No scientists would expect that the human beings will survive another five billion years. When all the people on earth are dead, it is apt to say that the humans and the world are unborn and empty, though there is still a problem of who is saying this. People should not expect that the world goes on for each individual. We should integrate the time and space requirements into our thinking rather than our selfish requirements, that is, the self-preservation within the society and the survival of the fellow human beings.

One philosopher had a saying at hand that only ethics and the stars in the sky gave him a consolation of life. Bertrand Russell, another philosopher, taught that when a misery of life grip us, we should reflect the vastness of the universe and try to get a consolation, thinking our misfortune is unimportant. Mind Only (or Emptiness) gets more to the core of the problem and look at ethics, stars and misery as illusions.

Non-Ego or Non-Recognition of Self

Hinayanism and Mahayanism recognised this theory as most important among the Buddhist theories and devoted major energy for its expositions.

According to Dr DT Suzuki, who contributed to better understanding of Buddhism in the Western world, the non-recognition of self is, in essence, the same doctrine as Mind Only and the two theories are the other side of the same coin. Non-ego theory states that our conscious self, as we have known since our birth, in reality does not have any substance and entity. We cannot conceive the existence of an ego-soul apart from sensation, perception, imagination, intelligence, volition, etc., and therefore it is absurd to think that there is an independent individual soul agent which makes our consciousness its workshop. (Suzuki 1973, p. 147) This proposition must be quite incredulous to the majority of us who have undoubtedly believed that the mind is the sole source of human existence. We have been conditioned to think that we identify ourselves with our bodies and more precisely with our minds.

Mahayanism goes a step further than Hinayanism, and denies a noumenal conception of things, that is, the conception of particulars as having something absolute in them. Everything has no self-nature, that is, no atman. Thus Mahayanism proposes the doctrine of non-atman-ness of things, adhering to the impermanency of all (persons and things) particular existences. The Hinayanists uphold this idea implicitly. (Suzuki 1963, pp. 41-5)

Self or other expressions meaning the same such as being, living soul, person, organism, individual, one who feels, agent, thinking subject are mere words which do not have corresponding ultimate reality. This is true to all the other selves and they all do not have any reality behind them. The self is something uncreated. (Conze 1975, pp. 3, 191)

The Buddhists proposed various theories concerning self in an effort to provide a philosophically acceptable of what a person is.

The concept of non-self according to one theory does not deny the following attributes:

|bodily process

The person <
|
|　　　　|sensation
|　　　　|perception
|mental process<
|　　　　|impulse to action
|　　　　|consciousness

According to this theory, the person does not exist beyond the above attributes, hence self or I as ordinarily spoken of is non-entity (Koller 1985, p. 162). All things including humans are egoless and devoid of selfhood. The theory does not deny the existence of mind. (Suzuki 1930, p. 181)

The Buddhists do not deny the existence of empirical ego but strenuously deny noumenal ego. When they say non-ego they are referring to the latter, which they sometimes call self-essence or noumenon. The former is akin to flesh of the Christian doctrine. (Suzuki 1973, pp. 163, 165, 170)

St Augustine claimed that knowledge of one's own being, of one's own thinking, of one's own willing is not open to doubt; there is an ego that exists, knows and wills.

The Buddha realised the view of no-self as his attribute as the following utterance of his reveals:

> Therefore say I that Tathagata [the Buddha] has attained deliverance and is free from attachment, in-as-much as all imaginings, or agitations, or proud thought concerning an ego or anything pertaining to an ego, have perished, have faded away, have ceased, have been given up and relinquished (Koller 1985, pp. 161, 174).

Since the self and things are impermanent Buddhism teaches people non-attachment to the self and things (p. 238).

The Mind Only theory claims that the external world has no substance and is only a reflection of our mind. Non-ego theory further insists that our mind activity is also like a phantom or mirage: we cannot pin down the conscious self to anything substantial. The Buddhists don't believe that their thinking self has any identity behind it. Hence the true Buddhists are unperturbed in the least if their face is spitted or if they are insulted in any way, because they don't recognise their self really exists.

There is a similar concept in the Bible:

> I gave my back to those who struck me, and my cheeks to those who pulled out the beard; I did not hide my face from insult and spitting (Isaiah 50:6).

The ultimate reality of Buddhism, that is, the Mind Only and non-ego theories, is sometimes expressed as Emptiness. All things are empty in that they lack a subsisting entity or self-being. What is ultimately negated in the teaching of Emptiness is the self and any self-substantiated entity.

Modern psychology supports the concept of non-ego theory. After 24 centuries from the Buddha's teaching, it proposes that the soul is an illusion. (Toynbee et al. 1968, p. 71)

I still don't know if the non-ego theory is correct or not in the physical sphere. If we are hit, we feel pains whether we believe in this theory or not. If we are hungry, we want something to eat to escape misery. How can we resolve this difficulty? Do we have to pretend that the problem does not exist? It does not look natural to me that under the physical sufferings we say that our egos do not exist. The Buddhists do not deny that we have sensation as I stated earlier, which seems to resolve this difficulty. Many religious fanatics courageously try to overcome the physical deficiencies. I, for one at my advanced age, cannot stand heat or cold of my surroundings and refrain from mental and physical hardships, though in my youth I did my best to try to overcome these difficulties.

We have to understand that the religions are about the laws of our minds and are not about the creation of the world, our body or the medical laws.

The biological evidence gives mixed blessings to the non-ego theory. A human contains as many as 10 000 billion cells. Our body cells, generally, are continually dying to be replaced by new cells, at a rate of some 50 million cells per second. Certainly various tissues have different rate of replacement: the cells lining the intestinal walls are replaced virtually every day while the nerve cells cannot be replaced. Thus we don't have the body we can call our own since its cells are all the time dying though our thinking brain which is made of the nerve cells remain the same identity through our life. When we are dead, nothing belongs to us since all the cells of our body and brain are dead and there is nothing to recognise ourselves.

Non-recognition of self goes against the law of preservation of moral conducts that is the fundamental teaching of Buddhism as well as of Christianity, though I point out in chapters 2 and 3 of this book that the morals are not really the core theories of these two religions. The religious doctrines are undoubtedly based, in part at least, on the premise that our daily behaviours bear fruits in the time to come: good fruits for good conducts and bad fruits for bad conducts. Many ancient people noticed this rather strange phenomenon and some of them had to rely on the concept of deity to explain them. This is a universal law beyond time and space, and is comparable to the conservation of energy in the physical world. The non-ego theory goes against this fundamental law of our daily experience. If we don't recognise our soul, the rewards and punishments of our thoughts lose all the meanings and we are left with a great puzzle which we cannot extract ourselves from.

'I think, therefore I am' is the famous philosophical remark by Descartes. In search of truth, he reasoned that everything--God, the world, his own body--might be all illusions. However hard he tried, he could not beat the above introspection on any account and set it as the first principle of philosophy. (Williams 1978, p. 72) Non-recognition of self by the Buddhists goes against the premise of this proposition.

As long as the believers treat the theory as theory, they may not have serious social problems. I am certain that people would esteem anybody who practises the Buddhist doctrine of non-ego to the letter as mad.

Section 3 Similar Concepts as Mind Only (or Emptiness) in History

We cannot prove that Mind Only (or Emptiness) correctly mirrors the real state of the affairs, as much as we cannot with many, possibly all, of the philosophical propositions. It is up to us to convince ourselves of the correctness of the view and integrate it into our way of thinking. Mind Only (or Emptiness) is certainly not a metaphysical concept but is an idea which reflects life and the world and finds its usefulness in our daily life, as the Buddha insisted his teachings to be so. The view has a universal application rather than restricted to the hierarchy of the monks. Hence many people in human history have expressed similar opinions to the concept. I am going to refer to some views which I have found related. The following is neither a systematic nor exhaustive list but I happened to come across, and is not referred to or not elaborated in expounding the doctrine in the last section. The relationships of these views to Mind Only (or Emptiness) are not necessarily clear cut and not easy to explain, and I hope readers should satisfy themselves by putting the inputs of their own.

- Objectivity of Views

  ME Montaigne in his *Essays* wondered about an identification problem of an individual by name. If another man with the same name as his lived and died, how can the later generation distinguish the two individuals? (Montaigne 1965, pp. 203-4, 475) The conclusion by Mind Only (or Emptiness) is that we cannot set apart the two, while they are alive and much less when they are dead. Certainly we can identify them legally and bodily with the help of photographs, videos, finger prints and DNA techniques, but not in the way Montaigne was querying about.

  This viewpoint has intrigued a large number of people through the history and it may be looking at people objectively, not relying on any particular person. If we look at the world objectively, an individual can be liberated from various constraints imposed on him or her. There are the haves and the have-nots in the society and the latter can derive some consolation by thinking that the view the third party makes would be such that the haves and the have-nots are projected in an objective picture and people cannot differentiate between the two in a subjective fashion: it is not important whatsoever who are the haves and the have-nots. The haves may have wealth, fame, power, physical beauty, or whatever the general public covet.

  As far as I am aware, some people have used this objective perspective negatively as the last paragraph describes. The concept does not seem to have seeds of any deeper significance to develop into a new way of thinking, though a large number of people have shown a strong interest in the idea.

  We must lead a certain way of life or go through a great suffering before we can be induced to the high contemplative state of mind to introduce a new way of life. Montaigne repeatedly wrote in his book that everything was in vain and he felt futile whatever he did (e.g., pp. 328, 330, 360, 721, 756, 849). As far as I understand he led a life which deserved to feel futile. He often did not live in the strict measure according to the philosophy he cultivated. In fact he wrote: The lofty and exquisite ideas of philosophy are found to be inept in practice (p. 511); He was born for company and friendship (p. 625); He had no other aim but to live and merry, and would run from one end of the world to the other to seek out one good year of pleasant and cheerful tranquillity (p. 640). I feel certain that a man like Montaigne who followed sensual pleasure as a daily routine would not be able to answer his query even to his satisfaction.
- Plato put out his famous theory that ideas alone are real and phenomena only the reflection of them.
- Protagoras, a fifth century BC Greek sophist who taught in Athens, made the following

statements: Man is the measure of all things; What seems to each man is true for each man (p. 443). He was emphasising the relativity and subjectivity of all what he saw around him. According to him, nothing is good or bad, beneficial or harmful in itself but so only in relation to a particular objective.

- I remember the gist of an essay which was a study topic of English at high school. I have reconstructed it as best I could:

> Life is neutral and colourless so to speak. We take out from life what we put into it. Everything is there for us to dig out according to what we believe. It is entirely up to us to shape our life.

- Marcus Aurelius (AD 121-180), the most philosophical Roman Emperor, made the following observation:

> If you are disturbed by anything external, the pain is not so much due to the thing itself but your assessment of it; and this you have the power to revoke at any moment (*The World Book* 1981, p. 334).

- Shakespeare (1564-1616) read, through the mouth of protagonist, Prospero in *Tempest* (1611), the following poem, which indicates to me the concept akin to Mind Only (or Emptiness):

> And, like the baseless fabric of this vision,
> The cloud-capp'd towers, the gorgeous palaces,
> the solemn temples, the great globe itself,
> Yea, all which it inherit, shall dissolve
> And, like this insubstantial pageant faded,
> Leave not a rack behind. We are such stuff
> As dreams are made on, and our little life
> is rounded with a sleep.
> (Elkins, Kendall & Willingham 1982, p. 177)

Shakespeare wrote the above verses towards the end of his life.

He also wrote the following verse in another book: There is nothing either good or bad but thinking makes it so.

He made no distinction between the reality and the dream in *A Midsummer Night's Dream* (1595). He humorously narrated there was no difference between a reality and a dream. What people believe in is no better than dreams and often their seriousness in the belief is quite illogical and comical.

It is interesting to note that Shakespeare, often being touted as the greatest poet humans have ever produced, expressed his conviction that everything is after all an illusion, that is, the concept of Mind Only (or Emptiness) of the Buddhist literature, in some of his works in his own way. He must have known that everything including his poems and even his existence was an illusion.

- 'Observe this simple counsel of perfection: Forsake all, and you shall find all. Renounce desire, and you shall find peace.' (Thomas A Kempis 1952, p. 137) This author of *The Imitation of Christ* believed that by discarding everything--wealth, fame, pride, etc.--he would gain everything and thus obtain inward happiness. This attitude comes from the notion that everything in the world is illusory.
- I still remember my high school teacher of history, stressing that politics is, or ought to be, more important than sports. He believed that politics has many important consequences

than sports. In the light of the Mind Only (or Emptiness) theory, he was wrong: politics and sports are the same in that both have no substantial consequences and both are illusions.

Some people indulge in politics quite seriously in the same way some people do in sports. Politics and sports have no value except for what appears to the minds of the people engaged and nothing more. Some people live for politics, which is no different from living for sports.

Politics is more important than sporting, singing, or starring in the movies. Politicians are more important than sportspeople, singers or movie stars. Production of consumer goods is more important than consumption of them. All the above statements are false according to the Mind Only (or Emptiness) concept.

- "Zhuangzi (Chuang-tzu) (c. 369-286 BC), a Daoist, fell asleep and dreamed that he was a butterfly, fluttering about and enjoying himself. When he suddenly awoke, he did not know whether he was Chuang-tzu dreaming that he was a butterfly or a butterfly dreaming that he was Chuang-tzu! To him human life was a 'Great Dream'." (Guisso & Pagani 1989, p. 105) He claimed that the judgment about values and distinctions are subjective and therefore relative.
- Friedrich Nietzsche wrote: There are no facts, only interpretations (Irmscher 1981, p. 352). He also wrote: The continuous repetition of a dream may well turn it into a reality felt and judged (Rietbergen 1998, p. xvii).
- According to relativity theory by Albert Einstein, space and time are not absolute, but relative to the observer, and both are interwoven into what Einstein called a four dimensional space-time continuum. Neither space nor time had an existence independent of human experience. As Einstein later explained simply to a journalist: 'It was formerly believed that if all material things disappear out of universe, time and space would be left. According to the relativity theory, however, time and space disappear together with the things'. (Spielvogel 1991, p. 872)
- Homer read the following poem:

> The day will come when this imperial Troy,
> And Priam's race, and Priam's royal self,
> Shall in one common ruin be o'erthrown.
>
> (Harbottle 1897, p. 376)

- Pyrrho: Things are not in nature, but only seem to be, as they appear to the senses (p. 436).
- St Augustine: They have suffered just so much as they have given in to pain. Montaigne: We feel a surgeon's cut with the razor more than ten sword strokes in the heat of combat. (Montaigne 1965, p. 39)
- Xerxes was feeling overjoyed by the multitude of his forces, the expeditionary force against Greece, at the Hellespont (Dardanelles). Suddenly he realised that this immense number of soldiers would give out within a century, and he knitted his brows and was saddened even to tears. (p. 174)
- 'Just as health, beauty, strength, riches, and all that is called good, as Plato says, are as much an evil to the unjust man as a good to the just, and the evil contrariwise.' (p. 192)
- Life is like a theatre, where the worst men often get the best places [Aristonymus] (Harbottle 1897, p. 371).
- Though Sigmund Freud was a Jew, he was an avowed atheist. He made the following observations in *The Future of an Illusion* published in German language in 1927. He reaches the conclusion that religion is not truth but an illusion. He further poses questions if the other cultural assets may be illusions: the relation between sexes may be disturbed by an erotic illusion; the political regulations and the external reality we can know through

science may also be all illusions. He makes a positive statement that science has given us evidence by its numerous and important successes that it is no illusion. However, religion is an instinct restrainer and has built civilisation hence it may be better to retain the religious teaching in the educational system, though he also puts up a theory that humans may be better off without religion altogether. (Freud 1989, pp. 43-45, 66, 70)

Reference List with Text Citations Marked

Breasted, James Henry 1950, *A History of Egypt: From the Earliest Times to the Persian Conquest,* Hodder & Stoughton, London.
46 (46) 46

Chan, Wing-Tsit (trans. and comp.) 1963, *A Source Book in Chinese Philosophy,* Princeton University Press, Princeton.
30 31 34 (34) 35 40

Chen, Li Fu 1987, *The Confucian Way: A New and Systematic Study of 'The Four Books',* trans. Shih Shun Liu, KPI Ltd, London.
31 (31) (31) (31) (31) (31) (31) (31) (31) (31) 35 (35) 38 85

Chien, Szuma 1979, *Selections from Records of the Historian,* this book is generally known as *Shih Chi,* trans Yang Hsien-yi and Gladys Yang, Foreign Languages Press, Peking.
9 30 (30) (30) 40 41 44 44

Conze, Edward (trans. and ed.) 1975, *The Large Sutra on Perfect Wisdom; With the Divisions of the Abhisamayalankara,* University of California Press, Berkeley.
82 94

Cotterell, Arthur (ed.) 1993, *The Penguin Encyclopedia of Classical Civilizations,* Penguin Group, Hong Kong.
19 86

Cotterell, Arthur & Morgan, David 1975, *China: An Integrated Study,* Harrap, London.
35 36 (36) (36) (36)

Davison, Michael Worth (ed.) 1993, *When, Where, Why and How It Happened,* Reader's Digest, London.
18 25 25 46 78

Ebrey, Patricia Buckley 1996, *The Cambridge Illustrated History of China,* Calmann & King Ltd, London.
29 32 33

The Editors of Time-Life Books 1988, *The March of Islam: Time-Life History of the World AD 600-800,* Time-Life Books, Amsterdam.
18 24 (24) 25 25 25 33 (33)

Eliade, Mircea 1978, *From the Stone Age to the Eleusinian Mysteries,* A History of Religious Ideas, vol.1, trans. Willard R Trask, University of Chicago Press, Chicago.
6 16 (16) 17 19 42 46 55

-----1982, *From Gautama Buddha to the Triumph of Christianity,* A History of Religious Ideas, vol. 2, trans. Willard R Trask, University of Chicago Press, Chicago.
6 6 10 (10) (10) (10) 17 (17) (17) 43 67 69 74 77 87

-----1985, *From Muhammad to the Age of Reforms,* A History of Religious Ideas, vol. 3, trans Alf Hiltebeitel and Diane Apostolos-Cappadona, University of Chicago Press, Chicago.
26 (26) 41 48

Elkins, WR; Kendall, JL & Willingham, JR 1982, *Literary Reflections,* 4th edn, McGraw-Hill Book Co, New York.

98

Flaceliere, Robert 1965, *Greek Oracles,* trans. Douglas Garman, Elek Books Ltd, London.
20 22

Freeman, Charles 1996, *Egypt, Greece and Rome: Civilizations of the Ancient Mediterranean,* Oxford University Press, New York.
48

Freud, Sigmund 1982, *The Interpretation of Dreams,* trans. and ed. James Strachey, George Allen & Unwin Ltd, London.
20

-----1989, *The Future of an Illusion,* trans. and ed. James Strachey, WW Norton & Company, New York.
100

Guisso, RWL & Pagani, C 1989, *The First Emperor of China,* ed. D Miller, Sidgwick & Jackson, London.
99

Guthrie, WKC 1969, *A History of Greek Philosophy,* vol. 3, Cambridge University Press, Cambridge.
19 (19) 21 (21) (21) 47

-----1975, *A History of Greek Philosophy,* vol. 4, Cambridge University Press, Cambridge.
20 21 68

Hall, Manly P 1984, *Lectures on Ancient Philosophy,* Philosophical Research Society INC, Los Angeles.
47 85

Harbottle, Thomas Benfield 1897, *Dictionary of Quotations (Classical) or Classical Quotations,* Swan Sonnenschein & Co Ltd, London.
7 (7) (7) (7) (7) (7) (7) (7) 8 9 19 19 21 21 30 30 (30) (31) (31) 40 41 43 43 (43) (43) (44) (44) 44 (44) 44 (44) 44 (44) (44) (44) 44 (44) (44) (44) (44) (44) (44) (44) (44) (44) (44) (44) (44) 44 45 (45) (45) (45) (45) (45) (45) (45) (45) (45) (45) (45) (45) 46 46 54 (55) (55) (55) 58 60 (61) 68 71 (71) (71) 75 (75) (75) 85 93 99 (99) 99

Harris, Nathaniel 1999, *Hamlyn History of Imperial China,* Octopus Publishing Group Limited, London.
16

Hopkins, Jeffrey 1983, *Meditation on Emptiness,* Wisdom Publications, London.
84

Hutchins, Robert Maynard (ed.) 1952, *The Prince by Nicole Machiavelli; Leviathan by Thomas Hobbes,* Great Books of the Western World, vol. 23, Encyclopaedia Britannica Series, William Benton, Chicago.
16

Irmscher, William F 1981, *The Holt Guide to English,* 3rd edn, Holt, Rinehart and Winston, New York.
99

Janaway, Christopher 1994, *Schopenhauer,* Oxford University Press, Oxford.
71

Kennedy, Paul 1987, *The Rise and Fall of the Great Powers,* Random House, New York.
23

Koller, John M 1985, *Oriental Philosophies,* 2nd edn, Charles Scribner's Sons, New York.
17 23 29 32 (32) 59 (59) 60 70 71 74 75 76 95 95 (95)

Kung, Hans; Ess, Josef van; Stietencron, Heinrich von & Bechert, Heinz 1986, *Christianity and the World Religions,* trans. Peter Heinegg, Doubleday & Co Inc, New York.
18 19 28 40 55 (55) (55) 74 83 84

The Lankavatara Sutra 1932, trans. Daisetz Teitaro Suzuki, Routledge & Kegan Paul Ltd, London.
47 69 70 73 (73) (73) (73) 73 (73) 74 76 (76) (76) 77 78 81 (81) 82 82 (82) 82 83 83 84 (84) 85 (85) (85) 87 (88) (88) 88 88

Levi, Peter 1980, *Atlas of the Greek World,* Facts on File Inc, New York.
22

Lopez, DS Jr 1987, *A Study of Svatantrika,* Snow Lion Publications, Ithaca, New York.
74 74 82

Lopez, Donald S Jr (ed.) 1996, *Religions of China in Practice,* Princeton University Press, Princeton.
Reprinted by permission of Princeton University Press.
34 (34) (34) 38 41 59 84

McGreal, Ian P (ed.) 1995, *Great Thinkers of the Eastern World,* Harper Collins Publishers Inc, New York.
34

Marx, Karl & Engels, Frederick 1970, *Selected Works,* vol. 3, Progress Publishers, Moscow.
6 36

Mercer, Derrik (editor-in-chief) 1996, *Chronicle of the World,* Dorling Kindersley, London.
42 43 48 63

Milston, Gwendda 1978, *A Short History of China,* Cassell Australia, Stanmore, NSW.
30

Montaigne, Michel de 1965, *The Complete Essays of Montaigne,* trans. DM Frame, Stanford University Press, California.
15 19 19 20 21 42 45 56 57 58 (58) (58) 75 83 89 91 92 97 (97) (97) (97) (97) (98) 99 (99) (99)

Murowchick, Robert E (ed.) 1994, *China: Ancient Culture, Modern Land,* Cradles of Civilization Series, Weldon Russell Pty Ltd, North Sydney.
9 41

Narada, Thera (trans.) 1993, *The Dhammapada,* 4th edn, Buddhist Council of NSW Inc, Eastlakes, NSW.
8 44 44 44 58 60 70 73 (73) 85 89

Oliphant, Margaret 1992, *The Atlas of the Ancient World,* Random House Australia, Milsons

Point, NSW.
44

Ostler, Nicholas 2006, *Empires of the World: A Language History of the World,* Harper Perennial, London.
17 76 78

Randall, John Herman Jr 1976, *The Making of the Modern Mind,* Columbia University Press, New York.
3 55

Richards, PD & English, FW 1985, *Out of the Dark: A History of Medieval Europe,* Thomas Nelson, Melbourne.
25

Rico, Gabriele Lusser 1983, *Writing the Natural Way,* GP Putnam's Sons, New York.
37

Rietbergen, Peter 1998, *Europe: A Cultural History,* Routledge, London.
52 99

Roberts, Gail 1973, *Atlas of Discovery,* Crown Publishers Inc, New York.
39

Robinson, Richard H 1976, *Early Madhyamika in India and China,* Motilal Banarsidass, Delhi.
82 (82)

St Augustine 1907, *The Confessions of St Augustine,* trans. EB Pusey, JM Dent & Sons Ltd, London.
49 (49) (49) (49) (49) (49) (49) 49 56 61 71 73

Schopenhauer, Arthur 1962, *The Essential Schopenhauer,* George Allen & Unwin Ltd, London.
83

Sharma, Arvind (ed.) 1993, *Our Religions,* Harper, San Francisco.
Reprinted courtesy of HarperCollins Publishers.
6 29 32 33 35

Sheowring, William & Thies, Conrad W 1982, *Religious Systems of the World,* Ajay Book Service, New Delhi.
16 34 74

Spielvogel, Jackson J 1991, *Western Civilization,* West Publishing Co, St Paul.
6 99

Stcherbatsky, Theodore 1977, *The Conception of Buddhist Nirvana,* 2nd edn, Motilal Banarsidass, New Delhi.
72 (72) 74 75

Stryk, Lucien (ed.) 1982, *World of the Buddha: An Introduction to Buddhist Literature,* Grove Press Inc, New York.
71 73 86 88

Suzuki, Beatrice Lane 1981, *Mahayana Buddhism,* George Allen & Unwin, London.
75

Suzuki, DT 1930, *Studies in the Lankavatara Sutra,* Routledge & Kegan Paul Ltd, London.
78 87 88 95

-----1963, *Outlines of Mahayana Buddhism,* Schocken Books, New York.
83 (84) (84) 94

-----1973, *Outlines of Mahayana Buddhism,* Schocken Books, New York.
72 78 80 (80) 80 80 (80) (81) 94 95

Thomas A Kempis 1952, *The Imitation of Christ,* Penguin Classics, trans. Leo Sherley-Price, Penguin Books, Middlesex, England.
Reproduced by permission of Penguin Books Ltd.
20 56 (56) (57) (57) 57 60 (60) (60) (60) 61 89 98

Thomas a Kempis 1980, *Imitation of Christ,* ed. Paul M Bechtel, Moody Press, Chicago.
20 57 60 68

Thomas A Kempis 1982, *The Imitation of Christ,* With reflections from the documents of Vatican II for each chapter, St Paul Publication, Homebush, NSW.
48 68 70

Toynbee, A; Mant, AK; Smart, N; Hinton, J; Yudkin, S; Rhode, E; Heywood, R & Price, HH 1968, *Man's Concern with Death,* Hodder and Stoughton, London.
41 86 95

Watson, Burton (trans.) 1993, *The Lotus Sutra,* Columbia University Press, New York.
43 67 76 84

Wayman, Alex 1984, *Buddhist Insight,* ed. George R Elder, Motilal Banarsidass, New Delhi.
67 72

Wells, HG 1925, *The Outline of History,* revised edn, 2 vols, Cassell and Co Ltd, London.
36 39 48 (49) 68

-----1971, *The Outline of History,* Cassell & Co Ltd, London.
68

Whitehouse, Ruth & Wilkins, John 1986, *The Making of Civilization: History Discovered through Archaeology,* Collins, London.
42 68

Williams, Bernard 1978, *Descartes: The Project of Pure Enquiry,* Penguin Books Ltd, England.
96

The World Book 1981, *The World Book Complete Word Power Library,* 2 vols, World Book-Childcraft International Inc, Chicago.
98

Yoshinori, Takeuchi (ed.) 1994, *Buddhist Spirituality: Indian, Southeast Asian, Tibetan, Early Chinese,* Cross Road, New York.
80 80

Index

Abbasid dynasty, 26
  Mongol conquest of Bagdad, 26
Aboriginal people of Australia, 63
Abu Bakr, 25
Aeschylus, 43, 45
Aesop, 44, 45, 47
Akhenaton (ancient Egyptian pharaoh), 46
  religious revolution, 46
Amenemhet I (ancient Egyptian king), 46
Amon (Amen or Amun), 46
Anon, 44, 45
Antiphanes, 44
Apostle Saint Mark, 61
Arabs, the, 25
  knowledge from the Byzantine and Persian empires to Greeks and Romans, 25
Ananda, 67
Archytas, 21
Aristonymus, 99
Aristotle
  Ethics, The, 48
  middle path, 73
  morals, 7
Arius of Alexandria, 23
  Arianism, 23
articulate speech, 36
arts, 11
Asoka (Mauryan Emperor), 90
Asshur (Assur); the highest god among the Pantheon in Assyria, 16
Aurelius, Marcus (Roman Emperor), 98
Aztec (Mexican), the, 39, 42
  Huitzilopochtli (the sun god), 39, 42
    wholesale human sacrifices, 39, 42

Baal, 46
Bhagavad-Gita, 17
Bible, the, 52-62, 73
birth of religion in primitive peoples, 12
Bloody Mary, 11
Bodhidharma, 88
  father of Ch'an School Buddhism, 88
Book of Documents (or *Classic of History*), 41
Brahmanism
  Samkhya, 18
  Vedanta, 18
  Yoga, 18
Buddha, the
  discoursing and self-realisation, 74, 84
  Gautama Siddhartha, 68, 76
  middle path, 72
  non-conformance of three faculties, 73, 82, 85, 86
    ego-soul, sense organs and objective world, 82, 85, 86
    no value in all man-made objects, 86
  Pali (colloquial language), 76
  prohibition of intoxicating liquids, gambling and sex, 87

  prohibition to fame, power, wealth and sex, 87
  Sakyamuni, 76
  Sermon 'The Foundation of the Kingdom of Righteousness', 74
  Tathagata, 76
Buddha, the, and Jesus Christ as religious reformers
  Hinduism and Buddhism, 3
  Judaism and Christianity, 3
  rejection of racism, 3
Buddhism
  Amida sect, 47
  avoidance of lust, avarice and hate, 6
  doctrinal diversity, 67
  Eightfold Paths, the, 2, 69, 70
  Four Noble Truths, the, 2, 69
  Mind Only (or Emptiness), 2, 67, 69, 81
  nirvana, 72
  No-Ego, 2
  refuge in
    Buddha, the, 67
    Dharma, the (the Law, Teachings or Truth), 59, 67
    Sangha, the (the Buddhist community), 67, 78
  Theravada and Mahayana, 75
    language: Pali and Sanskrit, 76
    salvation; individual and universal, 76, 77
  Twelve Chains of Dependence, 69, 71
Buddhist councils, the, 75
Burchett, WG, 88

Canaanite (of Canaan) sacrificial system, 46
Cato, Dionysius, 45
Cato Major, 31
Ch'an, *see* Chan
Cheng Hao, 36
Cheng Yi, 46
Ch'eng Hao, *see* Cheng Hao
Ch'eng I, *see* Cheng Yi
Chilo, 44
Chinese reference to god
  Di (Lord) or Shang-di (The Lord on High), 10, 35
  Tian (Heaven), 10, 35
Chomsky, Noam, 37

Chou, *see* Zhou
Chou Tun-i, see Zhou Dunyi
Christianity
  faith or actions, 47
  God is love, 56
  Jesus Christ, 61
  Kingdom of God (Truth), the, or nirvana of Buddhism, 59
  mercifulness of God, 54
  unitary system of doctrines, 41
Chuang-tzu, *see* Zhuangzi
Chu Hsi, *see* Zhu Xi
Cicero, 7, 30, 58
Confucianism
  causes of calamities (natural and human), 1
  Dong Zhongshu (prime minister), 32
  guide for the family and bureaucracy, 32
  one tradition together with Daoism and Buddhism, 29
  ren; Love thy neighbour, 7, 30
  state philosophy, 32
  vested interest of ruling minority, 32
Confucius
  Analects (*Lun yu*), 40
  Annals of Tso, 40
  Five Classics, 32
    Book of Changes, The, 32
    Book of History, The, 32
    Book of Poetry, *The,* 32
    Book of Rites, The, 32
    Spring and Autumn Annals, The , 32
  Historical Records, 40
  Mencius, 40
  ren (jen), 30
Constantine the Great
  First ecumenical council at Nicaea (325), 24, 62
    Arianism outlawed, 24
    Nestorius condemned, 62
    Trinitarian statement upheld, 24, 62
Council of Trent, the (1546), 48
  justification by faith, 48
    Luther, 48
    St Augustine, 48

Daoism
  Book of Recompenses, The, 34
  Classic on the Way and Its Power, The, by Lao-tzu, 34
  epithets, the, 34, 35
  reign of Li family during Tang dynasty, 34
  Zhuangzi by Zhuangzi, 34
Delphic Maxims, the
  Aristotle, 20
  at least 147 in all inscribed in the temple of Delphi, 20, 21
  Socrates, 20, 21
Democritus, 44, 54
Demophilus, 30
Demosthenes, 46
Descartes, Rene, 96
Dhammapada, The, 44, 57, 70, 73, 84, 89
Dharmakaya, the
  God of Christianity in one sense, 84
  nirvana, humanisation of Dharmakaya, 84
Dravidians, the, 12
  Indus valley civilisation, 12

Ecumenical Councils
  Fourth Council (451) in Chalcedon
    monophysitism outlawed, 62
  Second Council (381) in Constantinople
    Arius condemned, 62
  Third Council (431) in Ephesus
    Nestorius condemned, 62
Elizabeth, Queen, I
  Act of Supremacy, the (1559), 11
  Act of Uniformity, the (1559), 11
  British Empire, the, 12
  Church of England, the, 11
  defeat of the Spanish Armada, 11
  end of religious wars, 11
  flowering of literature, 11, 12
Einstein, Albert, 20, 99
Engels, Friedr12, ich, 36
Euphron, 31
Euripides, 41, 45
Exodus, the, 47

Freud, Sigmund
  Future of an Illusion, The, 99
  interpretations to our dreams, 75

Gandhi, Mahatma
  love, the unifying force of all religions, 59
  Rig Veda, the, 59
great arts
  ancient Greece, 12
  China, 12
  Elizabethan era, 11, 12
  India, 17
  Jewish state, the, 14
great religions
  China, 12
  Greece, 12
  India, 12, 13
  Levant, the, 13, 14
Greek arts
  dramatists; Aeschylus, Sophocles and

Euripides, 12
establishments of alphabets and city-states, 12
justice, virtue and beauty, 7, 57
Peloponnesian War, the (431-404 BC), 12
Pericles, 12
poets; Homer and Hesiod, 12
sculpture and architecture, 12
victories at Marathon (490 BC) and Salamis (480 BC), 12
Greek religion
Hesiodic pantheon, the, 46
monotheism and polytheism, 45, 46, 47
Socrates, Plato and Aristotle, 12
Han-fei-tzu, *see* Hanfeizi
Hanfeizi, 33
Hesiod, 19, 44
Works and Days, 19
Hinayanism, 41
Hinduism
sacrificial cults, polytheism and monotheism, 41
Vedic tradition, 18, 83
Atharva-Veda, 18
Rig-Veda, 18
Sama-Veda, 18
Yajur-Veda, 18
ways of salvation, 55
yogi, 86
Hobbes, Thomas, 16, 28
Leviathan, 16
Homer, 45, 99
Iliad, The, 19
Horace, 44
Hundred Philosophers, the age of, 29
Confucianism, Daoism, Mohism and Legalism, 29

idealism
main component of idealism; Love thy neighbour, 11
similarity of idealism in Greek philosophy, Confucianism, Judaism, Christianity, Islam and Buddhism, 6
Imitation of Christ, The, 68, 89, 98
Inca Empire, the, 42
numerous religious ceremonies, 42
Indian Buddhism after the eight century
Burma, 18
Sri Lanka, 18
Tibet, 18
Dalai Lama, 18
Indian philosophy, 18
existence = suffering, 18
Indo-Europeans, the, 17
Aryans, the, 17
Indo-Iranians, the, 17
Indus civilisation, the, 68
Innocent III, 3
Islam
Jihad, 25
Kaaba (House of Allah), 26
Sharia, the, 26
Shiah (or Shia) and the Shiites, 26
submission to the will of Allah (Truth), 61
Sunni and the Sunnites, 26

jen, *see* ren
Jihad, 25
Judaeo-Christian-Islam
aniconism and iconoclasm, 57
monotheism, 46
God is Truth, 56, 57, 58
God, not people, centred, 53, 54, 55, 60
prepared to discard even morals, and families and friends, 55, 60
how close we get to God (Truth), 39, 60
pleasures and sufferings, 61
the same tradition, 62
Old Testament, the, 1, 22
Old Testament, the, and the New Testament, 22
Qur'an, the, 22
Judaism
anthropomorphism, 7
I am a jealous God, 7
birth, 13, 14
Canaan (the Promised Land), 27
only for the Jews, 23
time delay in punishment, 8
Yahweh, 7

Kabir, 43
Kongfuzi, *see* Confucius
Koran, the, *see* the Qur'an

Lankavatara Sutra, the, 47, 87
Lao-tzu, *see* Laozi
Laozi, 30, 34
Daoism, 30
Law of Moses, the, 60
Legalism
Book of Lord Shang, The (4th century BC), 34
first appeared in Ch'i, 33
Hanfeizi (Han-fei-tzu), 33
Li Ssu (First Minister), 33
Shi huang-ti (Ch'in emperor), 33
Leibniz, GH, 18
Livy, 44

Lotus Sutra, The (Mahayana canon), 43, 67
Lucan, 45
Lucretius, 45
Luther, Martin
  Ethics, The, of Aristotle, 48
  justification by faith, 43
Lycurgus, 43

Madhyamika-sastra, The, 71, 88
  Nagarjuna, 71, 88
Mahayanism
  Madhyamaka (Middle Way), 71, 81
    Aryadeva, 81
    Nagarjuna, 81
      Mulamadhyamakakarika, The, 81
  Yogacara (yoga practice), 76, 81
    Asanga, 81
    Avatamsaka Sutra, The, 81
    Lankavatara Sutra, The, 76, 81
    Maitreyanatha, 81
    Samdhinirmocana Sutra, 81
    Scripture on the Explication of Underlying Meaning, 81
    Vasubandhu, 81
Majjhima-Nikaya, The, 67
Mamluks, 26
Mani, 44
Manichaeans, the, 44
Manilius, 40
Marshall, Sir JH (British archaeologist), 17
  Indus Civilisation (pre-Aryan), 17
    Harappa (1921), 17
    Mohenjo-daro (1922), 17
Marx, Karl, 48
  evangelical stories in the Bible, 48
Mary, Queen, 11
  Price Philip (future King Philip II), 11
Mazdaism, 16
  Ahura Mazda, 16
Menander, 7, 44, 45, 55
Mind Only (or Emptiness)
  against social reforms, 90
  emptiness of subject and object, 82, 84
  growing old, 92
  prohibition of fame, power, wealth and sex, 87
  realm of senses, 85, 86, 87
  social problem, 89
  suchness, emptiness, realm of truth, the various will-made bodies, nirvana, 83
  world or life, an illusion and thought-construction, no values, 81, 83, 91
Mohism, 34
  Mozi (Mo-tzu), 34
Monophysites, 24
monotheism, 46, 47
Montaigne, Michel de, 15, 45. 57, 74, 83, 92, 97
  Essays, 74
Moschus, 85
Moses, 10
Mo-tzu, *see* Mozi
Muhammad
  Allah; the chief deity of the Quraysh tribe, the ruling tribe of Mecca, 25
  Kaaba (House of Allah), 26
  Mecca, 26
  submission to the will of Allah, 28

Neo-Confucianism
  Cheng Hao (Ch'eng Hao), 36
  Cheng Yi (Ch'eng I), 36
  Zhou Dunyi (Chou Tun-i), 35
  Zhu Xi (Chu Hsi's)
    compiled *Four Books*, 36
      The Great Learning, The Doctrine of the Mean, The Confucian Analects and *the Works of Mencius*
  Wang Yangming (Wang Yang-ming), 36
Nestorius (Syrian churchman)
  Nestorianism outlawed, 24
    Councils of Ephesus (449) and Chalcedon (451), 24
  Nestorians, the, 24
Nietzsche, Friedrich, 99
nirvana (transcendental freedom)
  deliverance from suffering, 72
  different levels of nirvana, 72
    nirvana through Mind Only (or Emptiness), 72
  suchness or Dharmakaya, 84
  void, 72, 78
Non-Ego or Non-Recognition of Self, 94-96
  Suzuki, Dr DT, 94
    non-atman-ness of all (persons and things), 94

objectivity of views, 97
oracle texts or oracle bone inscriptions
  earliest written records of religious observance in China, 38
Oriental Philosophies, 74
Ottomans, the, 26
Ovid, 7

Pascal, Blaise, 60
people during savagery
  family and band, 5
  hunting and gathering, 5
people engaged in farming, 5

family, band and tribe, 5
Perfect Wisdom Sutra, 77
Sermon on the Perfect Wisdom, 77
Periander, 44
pharaoh in Egypt, 55
incarnation of order, i.e., God, truth, light and justice, 55
Philemon, 58
Phocylides, 45
Pinder, 75
Plato, 12, 15, 17, 19, 20, 45, 60, 97, 99
Republic, The, 20
Plautus, 44
Pliny the Elder, 58
Pliny the Younger, 44
pogrom, 11, 23
Polytheism, 45
Prakrit, the, 17
prophet
adherence to idealism, 8
intuitions and genuineness, 9
Protagoras, 97
Puritans, the, 11
Pyrrho, 86, 99
Pythagoras, 19, 68, 93
Pythia (priestess of Apollo at Delphi), 8, 21

Quintilian, 44
Qur'an, the (the Koran)
charity, 38
made to suit the Arabs in many ways, 27
pillars of Islam, 27, 28
practical penalties, 53
prohibition on drinking alcohol, gambling and idolatry, 28
Ramadan, 24

religion as means of survival
absolute, the, the ultimate, God (Truth), 40
Absolute, the, God or nirvana, 40
building huge or elaborate monuments, 38
charity, 38
core theories of Buddhism and Christianity have little to do with idealism, 11
desire to survive of all living creatures, 43
every religion is truth, 58
fasting, 38
fear of death, 9
God (Truth), 1
prayer, 38
reverence to God, 38
Russell, Bertrand, 94

Sabbath of Judaism, Christianity and Islam, 6
Sacrifices of humans and animals
human sacrifices, 10
Moloch; a god of Ammonites, 10
Semitic, Chinese and Inca peoples, 10
non-consequential religious practices, 38
Saddharmapundarika Sutra, The (Mahayana text), 78
Sallust, 45
samsara, the, 18
Sanskrit language
Mahabharata, 17
Prakrit, the, 17
Ramayana, 17
Schopenhauer, Arthur, 83
Seneca, 7, 44
Sermon on the Perfect Wisdom, 77
earliest documentation of Mahayana, 77
Seton, Ernest Thompson, 37
Wild Animals I have Known (1898), 37
Shakespeare, William
Midsummer Night's Dream, A, 98
Tempest, 98
Shamanism, 9
Shang and Zhou rulers, 9
Shang dynasty, 38
Shun, King, 44
Sima Qian (Ssu-ma Ch'ien), 30
Historical Records, 40
Socrates, 17, 19, 20, 46
polytheism and monotheism, 46
Solomon, King, 87
Sophocles, 43, 44, 45, 55, 75
Antigone, 44
Ssu-ma Ch'ien, *see* Sima Qian
St Augustine
City of God, The, 50
predestination, 50
Manichaeism and Christianity, 49
Neo-Platonism, 55
St Francis, 60
suchness, 80
absolute and conditional, 80
syncretism in religion
Chan Buddhism
Daoism, 6
Christianity
Greek philosophy, 6
Zoroastrianism, 6
Neo-Confucianism
Daoism, 6

Tacitus, 7, 31
T'ai tsung, *see* Taizong
Taizong (Tang emperor), 33
True Vision (his reign), 33

T'ang, *see* Tang
Tangri (god or sky), 41
Taoism, *see* Daoism
Tathata (Suchness or Thusness), 80
Ten Commandments, the (the Decalogue), 6, 46
Theocritus, 19
Theodicy, 58
Theodorus (of Cyrene), 91
Thirty Years' War, 11
Toltecs, the, in Mesoamerica, 42
Torah, the (or the Pentateuch)
  written by Moses, 52
  written down during the reigns of King David and King Solomon, 52
Toynbee, Arnold, 68
  Study of History, A, 68
    Mind Only, 68
Tripitaka, The (Triple Baskets)
  Abhidharmma, the (scholastic treatises), 68, 77
  Sutras, the (Buddha's discourses), 68, 77
  Vinaya (monastic law), 68, 76
Trismegistos, Hermes, 58
Tseng Shen (disciple of Confucius), 32
  Great Learning, The, 32
Tung Chung-shu, *see* Dong Zhongshu
Tzu Ssu, *see* Zi Si

Umar, 25

Vedas, Hindu tradition, 18
  Bramanas, the, 18
  Upanishads, the, 17, 18
Vimalakirti Sutra, The (Mahayana text), 69
Vulgate, the, 7

Wang Yang-ming, *see* Wang Yangming
Wells, HG
  Outline of History, The, 67
  Time Machine, The, 91
Wen (Sui emperor), 33
Wudi (the Martial Emperor), 32
  setting up the Imperial University, 32
    Five Erudites of Five Classics, 32

Xenophon, 61
Xerxes I, 99

yoga, 74
  Oriental Philosophies, 74
Yoga Sutra, 17
Yu, 31

Zarathustra (or Zoroaster), 16
Zhu Xi, 36
  Four Books, 36
Zhuangzi (Chuang-tzu) (Daoist), 99
Zi Si (Tzu Ssu) (grandson of Confucius), 32
  Doctrine of the Mean, The, 31, 32
Zoroaster (or Zarathustra), 16

www.ingramcontent.com/pod-product-compliance
Lightning Source LLC
LaVergne TN
LVHW081150110826
845149LV00008B/1613